The
Sea Wing
Disaster
Tragedy on Lake Pepin

Frederick L. Johnson

First Printing
June, 2014

Published by:
Goodhue County Historical Society
1166 Oak St
Red Wing, MN 55066
651-388-6024
www.goodhuecountyhistory.org

Editing: Diane Johnson and Rita Thofern

Layout and Design: David Thofern and Diane Johnson

Indexing: Char Henn

Printing: Bang Printing, Brainerd, MN

The Goodhue County Historical Society and the author would like to
thank the Jones Family Foundation and the Red Wing Shoe Company
Foundation for their generous financial support of this project.

ISBN- 978-1-4951-1166-2

Also by Frederick L. Johnson

The Sea Wing Disaster

Goodhue County, Minnesota: A Narrative History

Sky Crashers: A History of the Aurora Ski Club

Uncertain Lives:
African Americans and Their First 150 Years in the Red Wing, Minnesota Area

Red Wing: A Portable History

Richfield: Minnesota's Oldest Suburb

Suburban Dawn: The Emergence of Richfield, Edina and Bloomington

The Big Water: Lake Minnetonka and Its Place in Minnesota History

Four women view the Lake Pepin landmark, Maiden Rock, from a steamboat about five years after the *Sea Wing* disaster.

In Memory of the
Ninety-Eight

This view, looking west from Barn Bluff, shows the Mississippi River channel at Red Wing in 1874.

Table of Contents

John S. Howard's Lake City-based steamer *Ethel Howard*
served Lake Pepin communities, as its 1890 time card
shows. The boat played an important role in the *Sea Wing*
disaster.

Diamond Jo Line provided regularly scheduled passenger
and freight service to upper Mississippi River ports,
including Lake City and Red Wing.

A large excursion steamboat, *G. W. Hill*, pulls into the
Diamond Bluff, Wisconsin, landing about 1916. Diamond
Bluff was home port for the smaller lumber-rafter, *Sea Wing*.

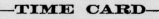

—TIME CARD—

OF THE STEAMER

ETHEL HOWARD.

Daily except Sunday. To take effect Monday, June 23, 1890.

Leave Lake City for Stockholm   9:00 A. M.
"   Stockholm " Lake City   9:50 "
"   Lake City " Stockholm   11:00 "
"   Stockholm " Lake City   11.40 "
"   Lake City " Stockholm   3:00 P. M.
"   Stockholm " Lake City   4:30 "
"   Lake City " Stockholm   8:30 "
"   Stockholm " Lake City   9:17 "

Will leave for Maiden Rock at 3:00 P. M.
Tuesday's and Friday's only.

Will leave for Pepin at 12:15 P. M. Saturday's only. Leave Pepin at 1:15 P. M., arrive at Lake City 2:00 P. M. Leave Lake City for Pepin 5:30 P. M., returning leave Pepin at 6:25 P. M.

J. S. HOWARD, Master.

EXCURSION AT
DIMOND BLUFF, WIS

W.H. BOURGHOLTZER
DIAMOND BLUFF

Author's Note

The Sea Wing Disaster: Tragedy On Lake Pepin is an expanded version of the Goodhue County Historical Society's 1986 book, *The Sea Wing Disaster*. That publication, with the addition of several new photographs, was reprinted in 1990. Both editions have been out of print for more than 20 years.

A narrow focus was employed in structuring the original book. It considered the events leading up to the disaster, the accident itself, and its immediate aftermath, within a time frame of about three weeks. Attention was given to the captain and crew, along with some victims and their families.

Discussions began in 2007 about broadening that first edition to include more content—photographs, letters, documents—that had come to light over the decades. Adding context and interpretation to provide a broader view of the shipwreck also seemed in order. In the summer of 2013 this project started to become a reality. Goodhue County Historical Society made the decision to move forward later that year.

Knowledge of the *Sea Wing* story has slowly grown along the upper Mississippi, but questions about the loss of this vessel continue to reach the historical society and author to this day. Novels have been written about the accident, and stage plays have been proposed on several occasions. A new 45-minute video about the steamboat's story, produced by Lake Citians, is due out in summer 2014.

Starting with the first review of the book's original version [Martha Bray, *Minnesota History* 50 (Winter 1986)], the *Sea Wing* disaster has been seen as Minnesota's own *Titanic* saga. There is, of course, no comparison to the scale and scope of that internationally-known catastrophe, yet, as Bray wrote, "the horror of [the Titanic] was no greater to those aboard than that experienced moment by moment by the passengers" on the *Sea Wing*.

Frederick L. Johnson
May 2014

NAMES OF PRINCIPAL LANDINGS.

0	ST. LOUIS, MO. †	28	FULTON, ILLS.
3	ALTON, ILLS.	26	LYONS, IOWA.
	CAP AU GRIS, MO.	30	SABULA, IOWA.
	FALMOUTH, MO.	31	SAVANNA, ILLS.
4	CLARKSVILLE, MO.	32	BELLEVUE, IOWA.
5	LOUISIANA, MO. †	34	DUBUQUE, IOWA. †
6	HANNIBAL, MO. †		DUNLEITH, ILLS.
7	QUINCY, ILLS. †		CASSVILLE, WIS.
8	LAGRANGE, MO.	36	GUTTENBERG, IOWA.
9	CANTON, MO.	36½	GLEN HAVEN, WIS.
10	WARSAW, ILLS.	37	CLAYTON, IOWA.
11	ALEXANDRIA, MO.	38	McGREGOR, IOWA †
12	KEOKUK, IOWA. †	39	PR. DU CHIEN, WIS.
12½	MONTROSE, IOWA.	40	LANSING, IOWA.
13	NAUVOO, ILLS.	41	DeSOTO, WIS.
14	FT. MADISON, IOWA.		VICTORY, WIS.
15	DALLAS, ILLS.		BAD AXE, WIS.
16	BURLINGTON, IOWA. †	44	LACROSSE, WIS. †
	OQUAWKA, ILLS.	45	TREMPELEAU, WIS.
18	KEITHSBURG, ILLS.	46	WINONA, MINN. †
19	NEW BOSTON, ILLS.	47	FOUNTAIN CITY, WIS.
21	MUSCATINE, IOWA. †	48	MINNIESKA, MINN.
22	ROCK ISLAND, ILLS. †	49	ALMA, WIS.
23	DAVENPORT, IOWA. †	59	WABASHA, MINN.
	LeCLAIRE, IOWA.	51	REED'S, MINN.
25	PORT BYRON, ILLS.	52	LAKE CITY, MINN.
	PRINCETON, IOWA.	53	RED WING, MINN. †
	CARDOVA, ILLS.	54	PRESCOTT, WIS.
	CAMANCHE, IOWA.	55	HASTINGS, MINN.
	ALBANY, ILLS.	56	ST. PAUL, MINN. †
27	CLINTON, IOWA. †		

† Coupon Stations.

This listing of upper Mississippi River landings, in order from St. Louis to St. Paul, is from the St. Louis & St. Paul Packet Company's *Local Passenger Tariff* book, April 1, 1882.

The portion of the upper Mississippi from Dubuque, Iowa, to St. Paul, Minnesota, is shown on this 1886 Diamond Jo Line Steamers' map.

Prologue

The Danger of Nineteenth Century Steamboat Travel

Captain William H. Laughton looked on impatiently as deckhands finished unloading his side-wheel steamboat *Galena*. The transfer of goods at Reads Landing on Lake Pepin's Minnesota shore left Laughton behind schedule. He asked his engineer for power to make a full speed run to Red Wing, his next stop. Passenger M. O. Everts watched the steamer's chimneys become "like volcanoes" during the voyage. About three hours later, sparks showering from the boat's smokestacks still flashed in the night sky as the packet moved past Barn Bluff heading for the Red Wing landing. As the steamer approached shore, glowing embers landed in bedding stored on the upper deck, flickering into flame. It was one in the morning, July 1, 1858, and some 70 passengers asleep in the ship's 46 staterooms did not know their ship was on fire.[1]

Flames finally burst into view, bringing cries of "Fire!" A ship's engineer roused crewmen, including Stephen B. Hanks, cousin and contemporary of the promising Illinois attorney and politician Abraham Lincoln. Hanks, an off-duty pilot on the ship, managed to get his pants on, along with one shoe and one boot, and rushed outside. He joined Captain Laughton in directing customers through a side exit and toward the boat's bow.[2]

Reads Landing opened as a Lake Pepin port in 1850. It became a busy stop for lumber rafters, like these shown around 1872. The *Galena* was traveling from Reads Landing on the night it was destroyed.

Galena's pilot beached the craft as the fire burned brightly against the night sky. Fortunately, the steamer's engines still chugged steadily, providing the determined helmsman power enough to keep the craft near shore. Many terrified passengers escaped over a narrow plank that had been extended to land. Others jumped overboard from all sides of the boat and swam to shore. The blaze burned to the ship's hull and then through it, sinking *Galena's* remains. Five people died in the accident.[3]

Red Wing residents lent aid to survivors—many were settlers moving to the new state of Minnesota—who, "having lost their all," were left destitute. Passenger Everts' graphic account of *Galena's* fiery end, published locally and nationally, etched the incident into Minnesota and Red Wing history.

Stephen Hanks, who became a Mississippi riverboat captain, grew hardened to such fatal events. He later wrote of *Galena's* demise, "Many such accidents have [occurred] on this great highway [Mississippi River] and this is but one of the series that accompanied steamboating from the beginning, and a mild one at that…."[4]

Nineteenth century Minnesotans, and Americans in general, understood the risks of steamboat travel. Highly publicized accidents, particularly those caused by boiler explosions and fire, attracted public attention. The great Mississippi "highway" Stephen Hanks knew had more than its share of misfortune. Statistics regarding such incidents, however, are inadequate. Until Congress established the Steamboat Inspection Service in 1852, no official data about these misadventures had been compiled. One study of steamboat mishaps occurring prior to 1840 reported 1,921 fatalities in 272 incidents.[5]

In July 1852, Cincinnati's *Cist's Weekly Advertiser* provided a compilation of losses on the nation's vast Mississippi River system, the waterway and its tributaries. This report analyzed the causes of 995 incidents. Snags—partially submerged uprooted trees—and other obstructions in the water accounted for 57.5 percent; explosion, 21 percent, fire, 17 percent, and collision, 4.5 percent, made up the remainder. Historian Louis Hunter's later evaluation of this report notes that if the *Weekly Advertiser* figures are used, "nearly 30 percent of all steamboats built before 1849 were lost in accidents."[6]

For those studying the *Sea Wing* event, such statistics are instructive. The *Weekly Advertiser* study found no instances of accidents directly caused by weather conditions. That 1852 analysis does not report any vessels capsizing. The snags and collisions denoted, however, could create enough damage to tip a ship over.

In June of 1902 the raft boat *Ravenna* became a rare victim of weather-related destruction. A tornado struck the Stillwater, Minnesota-based *Ravenna* north of Dubuque, Iowa, killing three crewmen. Annual reports from the United States Steamboat Inspection Service include steamship fatalities from vessels that "foundered in storm," but such incidents typically occurred on the Great Lakes or near ocean ports, not on rivers.[7]

A tornado struck the Stillwater, Minnesota-based *Ravenna* in June 1902, making it one of the rare riverboat victims of severe weather.

The *Sea Wing*, as did all upper Mississippi River steamboats, navigated unpredictable waters. The mighty river carved its own way south from its Minnesota headwaters to the Gulf of Mexico. In spring, particularly in times of flood, raging waters ran deep before slowing and randomly depositing snags, sand and silt. Drought, along with the ever-present sandbars and hidden shoals, presented additional danger to ships. The Mississippi could bring to grief even the most experienced riverboat pilot.[8]

In the mid-nineteenth century, Congress authorized the Corps of Engineers to improve navigation on the Mississippi by dredging channels and clearing snags. In 1878, the federal government ordered the Corps to maintain a four-and-one-half-foot-deep river channel. Such improvements made commercial and passenger steamboat travel safer for riverboat operators, including David Wethern, co-owner of the *Sea Wing*.[9]

A Ruger lithograph, c. 1870, shows Mississippi River channels from Red Wing's Barn Bluff. The "head of the lake," the northern beginning of Lake Pepin, is seen at the top center.

Wethern, the *Sea Wing's* captain, combined two careers in the Mississippi River town of Diamond Bluff, Wisconsin. Starting as a teenager, Wethern worked during the 1870s and 1880s on the river and at the general store he came to co-own. He spent the 1888 and 1889 shipping seasons piloting his new steamboat up and down the Mississippi. The ambitious young man gained sole control of his Diamond Bluff store at age 25. More merchant than sailor, he, nevertheless, had met the challenges that faced riverboat masters operating on the great waterway.

Lake Gervais Tornado: Harbinger of the *Sea Wing* Disaster

"At 4:45 [p.m.] it began to blow from the southeast and the typical funnel-shaped clouds began to form in the northwest, advancing slowly against the wind. As these clouds approached Lake Gervais they swooped down like an eagle, and in a moment the cottages on the south side of the lake were in the air along with trees and anything else that pleased the tornado's fancy...."[10] The advance of the deadly July 13, 1890, storm

On July 13, 1890, the Lake Gervais tornado struck north of St. Paul, shown in the foreground of these two photos. It killed six people before dissipating. Just over three hours later and 50 miles to the south, the massive weather system produced a frontal thunderstorm and straight-line winds on Lake Pepin as the *Sea Wing* steamed north.

described in this St. Paul *Daily Pioneer Press* eyewitness report was an ominous harbinger of a second more shocking incident a little more than three hours later: the capsizing of the steamboat *Sea Wing*.

By 1890, Lake Gervais, and Kohlman Lake to its east, had emerged as a popular vacation area for St. Paulites. The two lakes, located in the small French-Canadian settlement of Little Canada just six miles north of St. Paul, provided ample natural beauty and clean air. Visitors stayed at area hotels and cottages or camped in tents. For the most part, the July 13 tornado hammered Lake Gervais's south shoreline, claiming six lives. The "maelstrom of death," as *St. Paul Dispatch* labeled it, then swept "mercilessly" onward, injuring 27 vacationers.[11]

The vivid *Pioneer Press* account of the tornado's approach fixed in readers' minds the events at Lake Gervais. But locals and others would soon have more than a word description of the storm. From a safe bluff-top perch on St. Paul's West Side, photographer William F. Koester captured the twister's image with his camera. By chance, he stood on Cherokee Heights taking some city views when the storm muscled its way toward Lake Gervais, past the cameraman's lens.

The weather system that spawned tornadic winds at Gervais was not through with the Upper Mississippi River Valley. About three-and-one-half hours after the devastating tempest in suburban St. Paul, an extraordinarily strong frontal thunderstorm generated a violent burst of straight-line winds some 50 miles to the southeast. They bore down on Lake Pepin.

Captain David Wethern looked to the early evening skies and weighed his options. The havoc created by the windstorm that ripped through Lake City had just ended. Groups of passengers awaiting departure, joined by other onlookers, milled around his modestly-sized steamboat, *Sea Wing,* and its attached barge. His watch showed eight o'clock approaching. Delays would put Wethern's steamboat and customers well behind schedule and, no doubt, frustrate many of his guests. Yet signs of the storm front lingered. Some on shore warned of continued danger from severe weather. Was it now safe to take perhaps 200 excursionists back upriver? The experienced riverboat pilot contemplated one more factor: his wife and two sons were also onboard.

It was around eight p.m., just after sunset, on July 13, 1890, when Wethern, the Diamond Bluff, Wisconsin, merchant and *Sea Wing* co-owner, ordered lines cast off. He blew the ship's whistle and maneuvered away from the Lake City landing onto Lake Pepin. Captain David Niles Wethern, his passengers and crew, sailed north.

People survey the damage to cottages around Lake Gervais in the aftermath of the July 13, 1890, tornado.

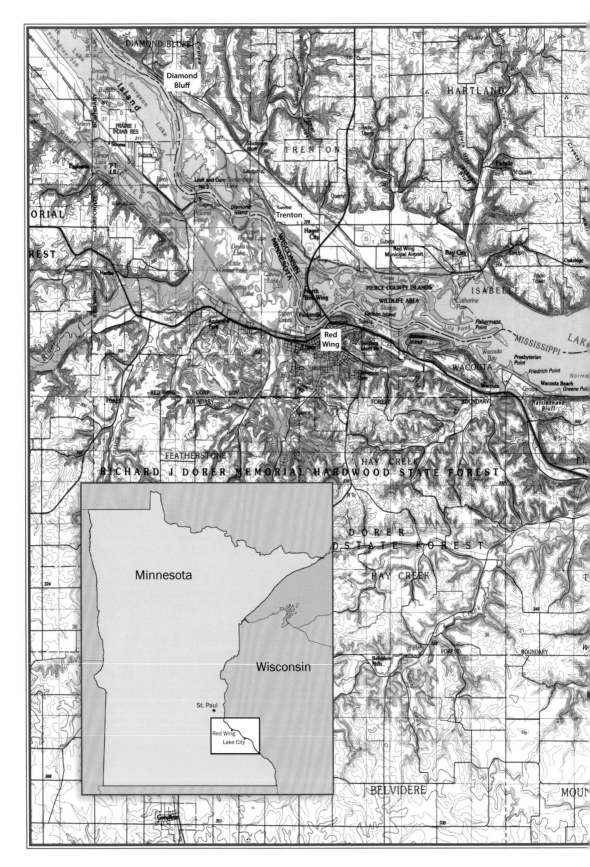

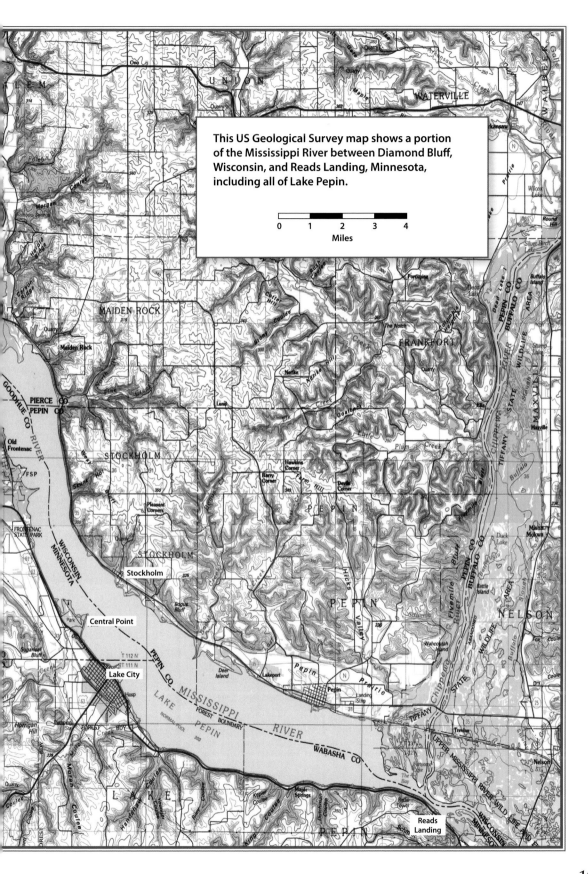

This US Geological Survey map shows a portion of the Mississippi River between Diamond Bluff, Wisconsin, and Reads Landing, Minnesota, including all of Lake Pepin.

0 1 2 3 4

Miles

Chapter 1
The Event of the Season

Sunday, July 13, 1890, dawned warm and humid, promising residents of the Upper Mississippi River Valley that the sultry weather of the past week would plague them at least one more day. It figured to be a busy Sunday for the crew of the *Sea Wing,* a 109-ton river steamboat based in Diamond Bluff, Wisconsin, 35 miles south of St. Paul on the Mississippi. David Niles Wethern, its captain and co-owner, had scheduled an all-day excursion down the river from Diamond Bluff to Lake City, Minnesota. The boat would stop to take on more passengers between these two points—at Trenton, on the Wisconsin side of the river, and at Red Wing, Minnesota.

Pleasure trips were not its usual duty; the steamer was most often employed as a log-rafter, one of many such vessels plying the upper Mississippi in the profitable timber and lumber trade.[1] Throughout the season, which opened in spring

and continued until ice blocked the waterway in winter, the *Sea Wing* towed rafts of newly cut logs to processing mills downriver.

The pleasure cruise was to be doubly entertaining for passengers who first would enjoy a leisurely 30-mile trip down the river on the *Sea Wing* and an attached barge, the *Jim Grant*. Once in Lake City, they would visit the summer encampment of the Minnesota National Guard's First Regiment at Camp Lakeview, where 13 companies of men were bivouacked.[2]

Wethern had scheduled the trip as one among his last as captain and pilot of the *Sea Wing*. He and partner Marion "Mel" Sparks had decided to sell the craft to interested parties in Quincy, Illinois, for $8,000, an acceptable price for a three-year-old steamer with a reputation as "unwieldy" and "top-heavy."[3] The stern-wheeler was six feet higher (22 feet) than it was wide (16 feet) and about 135 feet long.[4] Its flat bottom, like that of most commercial river vessels, made the riverboat capable of navigating the shallower sections of the unpredictable Mississippi.[5]

But the steamer's sale lay ahead, and on this trip the *Sea Wing* would shrug off its unglamorous commercial image for that of an excursion cruiser, complete with a barge featuring a deck for dancing and a small band for music.[6] The barge would be lashed to the port side of the ship's bow to facilitate passenger movement between the vessels.

The trip promised to be profitable. While the smaller Wisconsin towns of Diamond Bluff (469 residents) and Trenton (946) would provide some passengers, a crowd was expected to board at Red Wing.[7] After all, Company G, among the guard units at Camp Lakeview, was made up mostly of Red Wing men. A small advertisement in the Red Wing *Argus* three days before the voyage provided details: "Next Sunday the steamer *Sea Wing* with covered barge, Capt. D. N. Wethern, will give an excursion to Camp Lakeview. The steamer will leave Diamond Bluff at 7:30 A.M.; Trenton, 8:30, Red Wing, 9:30 and arrive at the Camp ground at 11:30 A.M. Returning will leave after the band concert. Hawkins' full string band has been engaged to furnish the music. Tickets for the round trip 50 cents."[8]

Sea Wing **Captain David Wethern**

The operation of the *Sea Wing* was a family affair, with seven members of the ten-man crew related by blood or marriage. Captain Wethern was a cousin of the three Niles brothers who came aboard to work on the Sunday excursion. Edmund "Ed" Niles, the oldest of the three at 21, was clerk and business manager of the steamer, while 20-year-old Will and 17-year-old Harry worked as deckhands. Co-owner Mel Sparks's wife, Ellie Niles, 24, and Millie Niles, 16, sisters of the Niles brothers, were also aboard for the cruise. Three of Sparks's brothers—ship's engineer William, deckhand Warren, and Jesse, who was along for the ride—were also on the ship. Unofficial hostess for the excursion was the captain's wife of 13 years, Nellie Boyes Wethern. She brought with her their two sons, Roy, 10, and Perley, 8.[9]

This view of Diamond Bluff and the Mississippi, c. 1900, was taken from a river bluff overlooking the village.

Also boarding at Diamond Bluff was Francis Gartland, depot agent for the Burlington Railroad. A 22-year-old native of Attica, New York, he had moved west to learn railroading and had been stationed at Diamond Bluff for two years. Gartland had hoped that Fanny Miller would join him for the trip down the Mississippi, but holding to strict observance of the Sabbath, Fanny's mother did not allow it. Undaunted, Gartland arranged for Nettie Palmer of Trenton to accompany him.[10]

Marring the start of the Sunday outing were the humid weather and an itinerant preacher, Georgas, campaigning to discourage prospective excursionists. The "walking missionary," in Diamond Bluff for a week, had begun warning townspeople on Friday about the Sunday trip on the *Sea Wing*.[11] The nomadic preacher, well-known to the Niles family, had appeared at their home asking for shelter and was welcomed to stay. Tall, gray-bearded and about 65 years old, the evangelist impressed Ed Niles, who had a chance to observe the family guest firsthand. Georgas told his hosts he was of Greek parentage, and with his polished, solemn, sincere image, he struck them as well educated and refined.[12]

Two days before the trip, Georgas had told townsfolk of being forewarned that the *Sea Wing* would be destroyed by a storm on its voyage to Lake City and that many lives would be lost. The missionary was successful in discouraging excursionists: in charge of booking passage, clerk Niles dealt with several customers who returned their tickets after the warning from Georgas.[13] As Captain Wethern readied to cast off lines at Diamond Bluff Sunday morning, the imposing missionary was still trying to convince the passengers not to go. And if he were not employed on the ship, Ed Niles thought, he would himself remain on shore.[14]

At 8:40 a.m. Wethern edged the steamer and barge into the main channel and headed downriver toward Trenton and Red Wing. The ship carried 10 crew members and 11 passengers. Several would-be excursionists who had missed the boat watched the paddle-wheeler move out of sight.[15] Shortly after noon that day, Georgas packed up his few belongings and made the rounds of Diamond Bluff announcing his departure. The preacher predicted that within hours a violent storm would sink the *Sea Wing,* taking many lives. He could not bear to remain and share the sorrow of the townspeople.[16]

<hr />

The man in the pilothouse of the *Sea Wing* had some experience in riverboating, but he had other business interests as well. David Wethern owned a general merchandise store in Diamond Bluff as well as half-interest in the steamer. But his life had not been easy. The Wethern family, from Detroit, Maine, a small city in the south central section of that state, had been among the first to settle in Diamond Bluff.[17] In the 1850s Wethern's father, David Young Wethern, arrived in the river settlement with his wife Esther (Niles) and son David and began farming. Two more sons were born there. Young David got his first job on the river at age 13 when he helped out on a boat hauling wood for George Hampton during one shipping season. He later worked a season for his uncle, Augustus Mero, a prominent Diamond Bluff citizen also with roots in Maine.

On ths Mississippi, Steamer Glenmont and
Bow Boat with Log Raft in Tow,
La Crosse, Wis.

A log-rafter like the *Sea Wing,* steamer *Glenmont* is shown pushing a raft of logs on the Mississippi in this 1905 postcard. The small "bow boat" at the front provided extra power to navigate the river's turns.

Diamond Bluff is shown in this photo, taken around 1905, with the Modern Woodman Hall (present-day Town Hall) in the foreground, and Burke Store, the white building, at the center. David Wethern's store, with its rectangular white façade, is next in line.

Wethern's father left the Wisconsin homestead in the late 1860s, taking his family to Granite Falls, Minnesota, where he became a merchant. Tragedy struck on May 16, 1870, when the elder David Y. Wethern was shot and killed in a holdup attempt while on a business trip to St. Paul. Esther Wethern and her three sons returned to Diamond Bluff. There, young David went into partnership running three wood boats with his uncle Augustus, who was a successful grain buyer and livestock dealer. The enterprising Wethern soon branched out on his own, acquiring interest in a general store and warehouse. David Wethern and his business associate split their property after two years, and Wethern got the store. By 1880, 25-year-old David owned the village shop outright and had his own wood boat, too. When the building burned in 1882, he quickly rebuilt.

Principally a merchant, Wethern was still interested in riverboats, and in 1888 he entered into a partnership with Mel Sparks to build a timber-rafter, the *Sea Wing*. They used the steamer to tow logs downriver as far as Illinois during the 1888 and 1889 seasons. Wethern served as principal pilot in 1888, but he wasn't as active the following year, making just a few short trips. He looked forward to this 1890 Sunday excursion—a boatload of happy, paying passengers, combined with a family outing for his wife and two sons. As he guided the *Sea Wing* out of the landing, the tall, bearded captain had full confidence in himself as a riverboat master, even though he had largely reduced his time at the helm and listed himself in the census as "merchant."

⁓⁓⁓

Excited crowds, mainly young people in their teens or early twenties, eagerly awaited the *Sea Wing* at its two stops—22 passengers at Trenton and well over a hundred in Red Wing. The daylong cruise promised them escape from the oppressive heat of the preceding week. Professor Ozias Whitman, Red Wing's retired superintendent of schools and *Daily Republican* weatherman, had predicted warmer temperatures and showers and noted a humidity reading of 88 percent at 7:00 p.m. on Friday.[18]

Those following the weather earlier that week took note of a tornado that struck Fargo, North Dakota, on Wednesday. Nine had died in a storm powerful enough to blow a train from its tracks. On Thursday another tornado swept over New York's Lake Champlain, with casualties of one drowned and seven missing. It was part of a tempest ravaging the East from Maine to Pennsylvania.[19] These storms failed to dissipate the low-pressure area through the Midwest, and on Sunday, July 13, an "abnormal barometer depression" extending from the Rocky Mountains to Lake Superior showed only small variations in intensity.[20]

This photo of the five Adams children was later used in the composite image of accident victims. Willie and Ella flank the seated Mamie. The two children on the floor, Charlie and Myrtle, were not aboard the *Sea Wing*.

Captain Wethern brought the *Sea Wing* into the Trenton landing shortly after 9:00 a.m. Among the small groups preparing to board the steamer were three children of the town's postmaster and general store operator, Benjamin Way. Twenty-two-year-old Frank Way was there with his fiancée, Mattie Flynn, and two of his sisters, Ednah and Adda. At the dock with the Ways were their cousins Mamie, Willie and Ella Adams of Trenton, and John Adams, of nearby Hartland, one of Trenton's neighboring townships. The two Adams families ran successful farms. Allen and Sarah Adams lived with their children, including Mamie, Willie and Ella, in a new farmhouse on a hill overlooking a back channel of the river, while James and Rebecca Adams, parents of John, owned one of the most prosperous farms in Hartland.[21]

With everyone boarded, Wethern left the Trenton dock, winding his way into the main channel to head for Red Wing and the passengers waiting there. Red Wing, one of the state's earliest settlements, was a prosperous river town of 6,000. Built in the 1850s on the site of a Mdewakanton Dakota village, its name came from a leading chief of that tribe. Lt. Zebulon Pike, exploring for the US Army, had first mentioned an Indian settlement in the area during his Mississippi River expedition of 1805 when he met Chief Red Wing near the future city. By the 1870s, the rich farmlands surrounding Red Wing produced abundant crops, giving the town prominence as a grain port, and by 1874 its exports of wheat had earned the city a place, according to St. Paul newspapers, "at the head of the list" of the world's primary wheat markets.[22]

Several young couples waited at the Red Wing levee as Wethern eased the *Sea Wing* into position for boarding. A leisurely cruise through what some called the most beautiful and picturesque portion of the Mississippi promised them a relaxing, even romantic, trip.[23] The two Staiger sisters, Annie, 20, and Frances, 18, who lived on their family's farm in Florence Township just south of Red Wing, were taking the trip with Frank Lampman and Ed Stevens, both railroad men from Minneapolis.[24] For Randina Olson of Red Wing, the trip was something of an early honeymoon. Her fiancé, Alexander O. Anderson of Belmont, North Dakota, joined her in waiting to board the steamer. Their wedding day was to be Wednesday, July 16, three days hence.[25]

Other Red Wing citizens were making the trip a family outing. The biggest household boarding was that of Peter Gerken, who owned a drinking establishment in the rear of the first floor rooms at Fifth and Plum (known as Plumb at that time) in Red Wing. The 45-year-old saloonkeeper and his wife, Maria, took all five of their children. Henry, at 15, was the oldest. Emil, 13, daughter Alvina, 10, Amandus, 7, and George, 5, rounded out the family group. The Gerkens also had charge of their niece and nephew, Rosa and Johann Rehder, whose father, Claus Henry Rehder, was the band leader on the *Jim Grant*. Another city liquor dealer, John Schoeffler, boarded with his wife, Kate, and sons John Jr. and Frederick. Nine-year-old William, the son of Schoeffler's first marriage, stayed behind with his grandparents.[26]

Peter Gerken

Henry

Emil

Maria Gerken

Amandus

George

Alvina

The *Sea Wing* also carried a number of single male passengers as it pulled out of Red Wing at 10:00 a.m. Ed Niles did not keep an exact roll of those getting on the ship, but male passengers apparently outnumbered female travelers three-to-one.[27]

One prominent young man on the craft was Joseph Carlson, 21, son of well-known Red Wing businessman and civic leader Gustavus Adolphus (G. A.) Carlson. City alderman and chairman of Red Wing's city council, the senior Carlson owned Pioneer Lime and Stone Company, operating at both Barn and Sorins bluffs. Carlson led the way in making Red Wing the state's "Lime Center" by the mid-1870s. Handsome Joe Carlson, a wild, somewhat spoiled youth whose antics had included riding horseback down Red Wing's Seventh Street shooting at gaslights, presented problems for his parents. They had sent him to Shattuck School in Faribault, Minnesota, in hopes he would receive needed discipline.[28]

The *Sea Wing* and barge, *Jim Grant*, are pictured as they were configured on July 13, 1890. This photo is thought to have been taken during the 1889 season.

Passengers Knute Peterson and Theodor Horwedel had something in common—both were soon-to-be-married bachelors. The 30-year-old Peterson, traveling without his fiancée, was to be wed in eight days, while Horwedel, 27, awaited the arrival of his bride from Germany. Horwedel's intended was also onboard a ship—hers was in the mid-Atlantic.[29]

Two young boys on the *Sea Wing* were last-minute additions to the passenger list. Ten-year-old Lenus Lillyblad and a friend were on hand to watch the stern-wheeler make its midmorning stop at the Red Wing levee. The steamer was taking on ice for the hot trip to Lake City when the two boys were offered a free excursion for helping with the task. There was no time for the lads to notify their parents, so the decision to go was theirs. Lenus's father, Gust Lillyblad, owned a Plum Street grocery and clothing store and was a leading Red Wing merchant.[30]

Four unescorted young women found it hard to contain their excitement as the boat left Red Wing and slowly headed downriver. This was an occasion for the display of Sunday-best clothes, and Mary Leach, an 18-year-old student at Magnuson School of Sewing in Red Wing, and her three friends had decided to wear new dresses. Mary's, of the white lace popular in that day, had a black satin bodice. She carried a new black satin parasol lined in red and edged with a black lace ruffle. Like many other passengers, Mary brought along a picnic lunch. She was a boarder at the O. E. Kyllo home in Red Wing, and Mrs. Kyllo had helped her pack for the picnic, including a luncheon cloth and her daughter's initialed silver cup so Mary wouldn't have to worry about broken china.[31]

David and Nellie Boyes Wethern pose with their children. Perley is standing in front of his mother, and Roy is next to his father.

As the stern-wheeler paddled its way south and Nellie Wethern made coffee, some excursionists took out their lunches.[32] There was dancing on the *Jim Grant* to Henry Rehder's four-piece band (not the advertised Hawkins strings). Ed Schenach, a Red Wing stonecutter, handled the big bass viol for the quartet as the happy couples made their way around the barge's improvised dance floor.[33] With music, laughter and gaiety all around, the trip was proving to be all that Mary Leach and her friends had hoped for. The *Sea Wing* excursion truly seemed the "event of the season."[34]

Minnesota National Guard Camp Lakeview as it looked in the early twentieth century, with Lake City just beyond

Scenic Lake Pepin and its picturesque surrounding bluffs enticed visiting excursionists each summer. Little wonder a passenger on the *Sea Wing* saw the river valley cruise, followed by an afternoon of military exercises, as "the event of the season."

Chapter 2

The Most
Terrible Catastrophe

Passenger expectations for a Sunday afternoon of fun ran high as the *Sea Wing* neared Lake City and the camp of the Minnesota National Guard. The day before, Governor William R. Merriam, accompanied by St. Paul Archbishop John Ireland and their entourage, had been impressed by the First Regiment's soldiers. They reviewed the mounted battalions, some 360 soldiers. Red Wing's *Daily Republican* newspaper also spread the word that visitors spoke highly of Company G, the Red Wing unit whose men had a reputation as the "best entertainers" in the camp.[1]

Capt. Charles A. Betcher, commander of Company G, had his men ready for a full day. Part of a prominent Red Wing family active in the lumber trade, the 27-year-old was capable of putting on a show of his own. Betcher handled a rifle well, having earned a marksmanship badge ranking him one of the regiment's best shots. Visitors would observe the encampment and view several military demonstrations. A band concert and a dress parade also appeared on the schedule.[2]

But more than military maneuvers awaited *Sea Wing* passengers. The citizens of Lake City had gone all out to make certain a carnival spirit prevailed for what promised to be a most exciting day. Around both the town and the camp, popcorn, lemonade and ice-cream stands were set up to provide refreshments. A band playing lively music helped keep the atmosphere cheerful and light. The only negative note was the weather. Heavy, humid air prevalent in the region bathed the National Guard facility.

The military base, rightly named Lakeview, overlooked scenic Lake Pepin, a 21-mile-long widening of the Mississippi running from just south of Red Wing to Wisconsin's Chippewa River delta. Even those on board the *Sea Wing*, who hoped breezes generated by the ship's speed would cool them, took notice of the sticky air.[3]

Among the most beautiful in a region known for lakes, Pepin nestles between grass-and-tree-covered limestone bluffs rising to 400 feet. Its sparkling blue and comparatively shallow waters,

Lake City is shown about 1900 with Lake Pepin and the Wisconsin river bluffs in the background.

usually placid, attract many visitors. But the lake is subject to quick changes from tranquil and serene to stormy and turbulent, and it earned the respect and fear of rivermen making their living on the Mississippi.[4] As Captain Wethern steered into the area south of Red Wing known as "the head of the lake," he saw only the quiet blue expanse of a calm Lake Pepin. He continued toward Lake City.

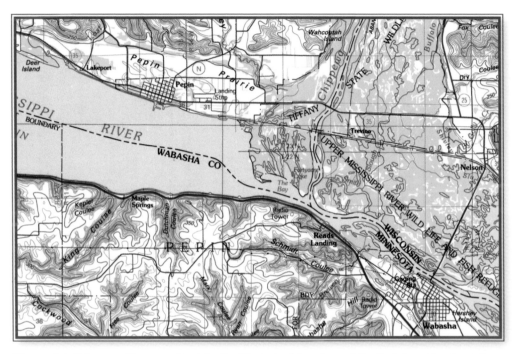

Wisconsin's Chippewa River empties into the Mississippi forming a delta that slows the river's flow, creating Lake Pepin.

Sea Wing excursionists weren't the only ones with designs on Lake City that day. Others went downriver in their own craft, among them Ira Fulton, a 37-year-old engineer who worked at Red Wing Pottery. Fulton invited friends aboard his own small steam yacht, the *Undine*, for the trip. Among his passengers, all Red Wing men, was city alderman George Cook, along with E. D. Morris, C. D. Jacoby, and Main Street saloonkeeper Fred Christ. The *Undine* had mechanical problems en route, and Fulton knew he would not be able to take his steamer home until after repair. But the Red Wing men were unconcerned about transportation—they could return home on the *Sea Wing*.[5]

Wethern's steamboat reached Lake City at 11:30 a.m., tying up at the Washington Street landing.[6] Though the captain had set the return trip for 6:00 p.m., co-owner Mel Sparks told passengers the vessel would remain at Lake City until the military doings were over. The *Sea Wing*, he promised, would not leave until the crowd returned. Thus, passengers left the ship, some on foot, but a majority making their way by horse-drawn "buses" toward the guard camp south of Lake City.[7]

A group of Red Wing residents visiting Camp Lakeview pose with local National Guard soldiers. Two officers, Captain Charles A. Betcher, reclining on the far left, and Major Arthur Pierce, standing next to the dark horse, played important roles in the *Sea Wing* accident aftermath.

Sea Wing passengers heading to Camp Lakeview looked forward to a display of cannon fire by a National Guard artillery battery, perhaps similar to this one from about 1900.

The First Regiment proved itself to be a good host. Soldiers acted as guides for tours of the camp facilities, which the visitors found interesting and informative.[8] As the afternoon wore on, gathering clouds suggested the approach of rain, yet they failed to dampen the spirits of the crowd. The four o'clock band concert went on as scheduled.[9]

Sixty miles to the northwest the weather front just beginning to menace Lake City had spawned a deadly storm. Dr. W. W. Routh, camped on Lake Gervais north of his St. Paul home, watched as a funnel cloud formed in the northwest and advanced toward the lake. Shortly before 5:00 p.m., a tornado swooped down on the south shore, almost immediately sweeping away cottages, tents and trees, leaving several dead and 11 injured. Others were missing; there was speculation they had been carried into the lake or their bodies had been hidden in debris along the shore. The final death toll was six.[10]

Starting near Snail Lake, where it pelted dozens of chickens with hail of "phenomenal size" at the Chase farm, the storm passed in a southeasterly direction, hitting Little Canada and Lake Gervais particularly hard. At the same time, a gale in nearby Hastings and Denmark Township in south Washington County uprooted trees and unroofed houses.[11] The people in Lake City had no knowledge of the storms raging to the north, but signs were clear that Lake Pepin might be in for a blow. From around 5:00 p.m., the sky indicated thunderstorms brewing both to the northwest and north.[12]

The First Regiment's military exercises were to conclude with a dress parade shortly after 7:00 p.m. At the end of the parade, *Sea Wing* passengers were expected to head for the steamer. But a rain squall upset the timetable and many in the crowd, dressed in their Sunday best clothes, scattered to find shelter. Mary Leach and her friends were among those taking refuge in a tent at Camp Lakeview. They talked and joked and forgot about the time as the rain beat down. But the Red Wing girls had more than rain to worry about. Still at the National Guard encampment, they began to realize

the *Sea Wing* might leave without them, and the reputations of unchaperoned teenagers forced to stay the night in Lake City might well suffer. When the rain stopped, the girls hurried to the boat landing. The boat had gone, stranding them—and all because they had not wanted to get their new dresses wet! Mary Leach could only guess what Mrs. Kyllo would say, and when she thought of the luncheon cloth and silver cup still on the stern-wheeler with her new parasol, she began to cry.[13]

Leach and her companions weren't the only people

Mary Leach and her friends might have taken shelter in tents like these. Red Wing photographer R. W. Hubbell took this image at Camp Lakeview in the early 1890s.

missing the *Sea Wing's* departure. Casper "Cap" Haustein and his friends, brothers Joseph and William Eisenbrand, along with William Becker, were among those stranded. The early evening wind and rain, plus a welcome invitation, delayed the quartet. A Red Wing guardsman called the young men into a tent where beer was being served. As Haustein recounted in a 1929 memoir, "When the boys went to camp, you could see half a carload [of beer] lined up on the [railroad] platform…." Haustein and Becker decided to "partake of the amber fluid." The two Red Wing friends then caught the next carriage back to Lake City.

Arriving at the landing, they found their ride home already out on Lake Pepin. The two friends also saw on the horizon, "…dark black clouds…so low you would think they'd touch your head." Haustein, undeterred by the ominous skies, grabbed a lantern, ran to the end of the dock and began waving the light, beckoning for the steamer's return. The riverboat continued to head up the lake. With a thunderstorm blowing their way, Haustein and Becker took shelter in a Lake City candy store.

—⁓—

Captain Wethern decided to leave Lake City under pressure and in the midst of changing weather conditions. When the first rain let up, he believed the storm to be largely over. Eager to start back upriver, he blew the ship's whistle to get passengers on board. Wethern discussed the advancing storm clouds with clerk Ed Niles, noting he expected it to "blow a little," but indicating his desire to make the run. Niles, who had previously been through two severe storms, had his doubts, and he observed it was just the weather for a cyclone. He wasn't the only one concerned. Some people at dockside tried to persuade the officers and crew not to leave the harbor. Others attempted to discourage friends from going aboard. In some cases they succeeded.[14]

Among the more uneasy passengers were Samuel Haskell Purdy and his brother, William. Samuel Purdy felt a strong premonition he should not go on the *Sea Wing*. In fact, he and William had tried to take the train back to Red Wing, despite their lack of funds. After some hesitation, the Purdys took up the offer of their friend Martin O'Shaughnessy to lend them money. They went to the railroad station, only to find the train already gone. So, despite Samuel's reluctance, the two Purdys were on the *Sea Wing*. O'Shaughnessy joined them.[15]

The captain and crew also heard from others eager to get home. Wethern estimated his passenger load had increased. The *Sea Wing* had taken on eight men from Ira Fulton's disabled yacht, along with two women from the steamer

Wanderer. Also climbing aboard were about five Lake City residents on their way to Red Wing. Wethern figured he had roughly 175 excursionists onboard as he made ready to depart. At about 8:00 p.m. the captain cast off the lines and started onto Lake Pepin.[16]

Some passengers had second thoughts when they saw the sky becoming more ominous. Charlie Sewall of Lake City, among the worried, took direct action. When the *Sea Wing* and its barge moved opposite the Sinclair Ice House in Lake City, Sewall said "Goodbye, boys!" jumped off the barge, and swam the 300-plus feet to

Lake City's Washington Street landing, taken about a decade after the *Sea Wing* disaster, looks much as it did at the time of the accident. The photo shows the Streckfus Company's steamer *J. S.* nosed to the shore. Lake City's original pier is behind the steamboat, extending into Lake Pepin.

shore. Even so, those in fear on the *Sea Wing* had little idea the storm pounding the landscape to their north and west was part of a system that had produced a killer tornado near St. Paul, or that the heavy weather was headed directly for Lake Pepin.[17]

Shortly after the riverboat's departure, the storm front muscled its way through Red Wing and its surrounding farmland. Winds ripped roofs from some houses, chimneys from others, and totally demolished barns. In the city proper, wooden sidewalks were destroyed and business buildings damaged, with hardly a street escaping unscathed. Many broken shade trees littered the city. Outside of town the storm picked an apple orchard almost clean. Farm fields were hit hard, with corn and small grain crops flattened as if they had been rolled.[18] Professor Whitman, the *Daily Republican* weatherman, recorded winds at his station from 8:12 to 8:15 p.m. of 60 miles per hour. After that, gusts blew the cups off his anemometer.[19]

The storm swept on. Moving southeast and with increasing intensity, it smashed into Lake City and Lake Pepin about 15 minutes later. In Florence Township, about halfway between Red Wing and Lake City, seven-year-old Mathilda Staiger and her family took cover in the cellar of their newly-built farm home. The sky had turned an alarming black and red, frightening the young girl and giving her no time to think much about her sisters, Annie and Frances, aboard the *Sea Wing*.[20] In Lake City, Mary Leach and her friends, still upset about missing the boat, were consoled by the young men who had now escorted them to the Washington Street landing. The men said they would get a horse and buggy to return them to Red Wing.[21]

Suddenly lightning flashed, rain fell, and Leach's little party ran for cover. Wreckage from buildings flew past as the young women and men struggled against the gusts. The sound of breaking glass and falling debris mingled with the cries of the townspeople. Leach, out of breath and traumatized by the storm, was pushed into a building. Others huddled with her. Lightning flashed again and again; as the building rattled, they heard bricks falling. Someone screamed. With a terrible roar the wind tore away the roof. It landed nearby with a terrifying crash. The Red Wing teenagers prayed and wrung their hands. Some, hysterical, sobbed and moaned.[22]

A group of First Regiment officers sat in "inky darkness" inside the hospital tent at Camp Lakeview as the weather system approached. Gusts of wind howled down the ravine between the high bluffs south of Camp Lakeview. A regimental history recorded what happened next: "Then for a moment all was still as death. Men rushed from their tents with axes and hatchets…to drive in their tent pins. In less than one minute…the cyclone struck us with all its terrific force. The hospital tent…went up like a balloon and then came down on its occupants like a big wet cloth that it was. The air was filled with flying tent poles, tent pins, fence boards, and everything movable moved. Not a light was burning in the camp, and between the flashes of lightning, the angry waves of Lake Pepin could be seen rolling mountain high."

Eight of the First Regiment's 10 mess tents blew down, and Lt. C. E. Metz later reported that the "cooks were about as scared as a set of individuals can be imagined." Col. W. B. Bend's tent soared aloft, and a flying steamer trunk struck the leg of the

A Minnesota National Guard officer took these photographs of Camp Lakeview before and after the straight-line winds of July 13. The "day after," image, below, shows the remains of the large regimental hospital, mess and service tents. Note that all but a handful of tents were blown down. The smaller ones seen here were reset following the storm. The stables where guardsmen sought shelter are near the lake.

First Regiment's commander, bruising him badly. The mounted troops, camped closest to the lakeshore and more exposed than the others, were fortunate to lose only three tents. Heavy rains caused foot-deep water on some of the tented city's streets. With "not a dry cot, blanket or coat" in the camp, the guardsmen, wet to the skin, retreated to the stables where they huddled together in the stalls. With medical supplies lost, two officers ordered horses saddled for a trip to Lake City where they expected to find replenishments.[23]

The storm gradually lost power. Winds died, the rain stopped, and calm settled over Lake City and its shaken inhabitants. Residents emerged from their shelters to assess the damage and found wreckage littering the streets. The Collins Brothers' saw and planing mill had been destroyed. Tin roofs lay in pieces here and there. Hanisch Academy of Music had suffered the most—its entire roof carried away. Part of the Lyons Block was damaged, and the Young and Companies Dry Goods Block had been nearly demolished. Thirty buildings in the small business area were in need of repair.[24]

Mary Leach and her three teenage girlfriends emerged from shelter to a scene of havoc. Through the dark they saw broken trees and branches, tangled wires and damaged buildings. Ahead of them was a man carrying the limp form of a woman. Stunned, the group stopped at a crowded hotel for some food and rest. Suddenly a breathless man burst into the hotel, creating a stampede with his news: "The *Sea Wing* has been hit by the tornado! It's sinking and they need help!"[25]

Indeed, the storm that had torn up Lake City had also pounded Lake Pepin and the crowded steamboat. By the time the winds came up, Captain Wethern had safely guided his craft and the attached barge nearly five miles up Lake Pepin. He believed his three-year-old boat was safe and seaworthy, and the storm would not be severe. And Wethern had just passed a boat from the Van Sant line whose captain was dropping a raft of logs at Reads Landing below Lake City. That pilot hadn't even mentioned the weather.[26]

A steady wind blew from the west off the Minnesota shore as Wethern steered his steamer toward Maiden Rock Point on the Wisconsin side. He intended to pilot the *Sea Wing* under the bluff and continue upstream along the bend. Then Wethern spotted a squall heading for the ship. He turned the *Sea Wing* toward the Minnesota shore to meet the storm head on. The ship tilted as he made the turn, and then righted itself. Wethern maintained his heading directly into the wind.[27]

The approach of the storm had not been lost on the excursionists whose uneasiness grew as clouds spilled over Point Au Sable. Ira Fulton talked with his friend George Smith, pointing to

The *Sea Wing* traveled past Central Point, left, toward Maiden Rock, right, as it returned to Red Wing.

the sky and predicting crosswinds. Fulton feared Wethern would not be able to hold the ship. "If this boat goes over," he warned, "we'll all drown like rats in a trap." Bass fiddler Ed Schenach was also alarmed. With waves rising and the sky darkening, the paddle-wheeler was pitching precariously in the turbulent waters. Schenach decided to cross from the *Sea Wing* to the barge.[28]

Only a few women rode on the barge. Earlier, some men had begun singing songs of questionable character, forcing many of the women to leave the *Jim Grant* and take refuge in the cabin of the *Sea Wing*. Ship's co-owner and chief engineer Mel Sparks quieted the men, who had been drinking.[29]

The *Sea Wing*, preparing for an earlier cruise, looks much as it did on the day of the disaster. When the steamer overturned on July 13, 1890, more than 200 people were on board. The cabin, behind the railing, was crowded with passengers when the boat capsized.

As it became clear the boat would be hit by the storm, word reached some passengers that Captain Wethern wanted all women and children inside the cabin. Those concerned about wind and rain had already sought shelter there. Then some crewmen, including Sparks, learned that Wethern had changed his mind and now considered the barge a safer place.[30] Nevertheless, most passengers already inside stayed there.

As Wethern steered the *Sea Wing* into the wind, two sharp gusts struck the vessel. All on board felt the shudders, and their fear grew. The boat, with its flat bottom, started to sway, rolling back and forth. Increasing winds rocked the 22-foot-high superstructure, each lurch cut short by a tug from the ropes lashed to the barge. The more the *Sea Wing* rocked, the harder the barge ropes jerked. Nervous passengers felt the ship was being pulled apart. During the boat's violent gyrations, Mel Sparks and his brother William, the second engineer, struggled to stand at their stations in the engine room. They were thrown to the floor as burning embers spilled out of the boilers.[31]

Alone in the pilothouse, Captain Wethern labored to control the boat. Still confident, he reminded himself that he had seen higher waves than these. Wethern's wife, Nellie, had been setting a good example for the passengers. Earlier, she had put eight-year-old Perley, tired from playing at Camp Lakeview, to bed in the captain's stateroom. Now, she sat in a rocking chair near the stateroom door.[32]

But the winds increased, and passengers rushed about, seeking shelter. Wethern ordered Ed Niles below to calm the travelers. The clerk found people crowding into the main cabin in hopes of avoiding the wind and rain. Niles then looked across the water, spotting a funnel-shaped cloud darting up and down in the ship's path just 500 yards away.[33]

To the rear in back of the cabins stood George Diepenbrock, Jr., son of a Red Wing justice of the peace. The young Diepenbrock had donned a life preserver and was standing in the small galley. With him were Fred and Lizzie Hempftling, Mary Hempftling's two teenagers. Other passengers were tying on cork or tule life preservers carried aboard ship. The barge passengers also saw the storm clouds and took what cover they could as a violent gust swept chairs, band instruments and decorations from the upper deck of the *Jim Grant*. Lightning flashed, and those aboard the *Sea Wing* saw low, dark clouds rushing toward them. Many began to pray.[34]

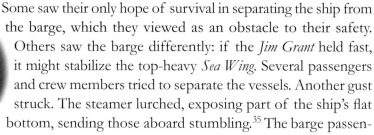

Some saw their only hope of survival in separating the ship from the barge, which they viewed as an obstacle to their safety. Others saw the barge differently: if the *Jim Grant* held fast, it might stabilize the top-heavy *Sea Wing*. Several passengers and crew members tried to separate the vessels. Another gust struck. The steamer lurched, exposing part of the ship's flat bottom, sending those aboard stumbling.[35] The barge passengers watched in horror as the *Sea Wing* tipped to a 45-degree angle, balanced an instant, then turned over completely.[36]

Mary Hempftling, center, and her teenaged children, Lizzie and Fred Jr.

The scene was a nightmare. Struggling in the turbulent waters or battling to free themselves from being trapped inside the cabins, more than a hundred passengers fought for their lives. A few surfaced, attempting to gain safety on the slippery hull. Those huddled on the barge could only look on helplessly as a virtual canopy of lightning illuminated the lake and the struggles of those sinking beneath Pepin's waters.

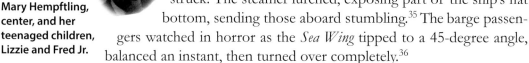

A St. Paul *Pioneer Press* artist depicted the *Sea Wing* in trouble, with the barge *Jim Grant* breaking free. The illustration was used with a 1926 story about Capt. David Wethern.

Chapter 3
The Terrifying Reality

Those passengers floundering in the water immediately following the *Sea Wing's* sudden roll proved to be the lucky ones. The strong swimmers among them had a chance for survival. For excursionists trapped inside the capsized riverboat, escape was almost impossible. Still, some were fighting to get out.

George Diepenbrock had headed from the galley to the railing outside when the *Sea Wing* began to tip, but then returned inside. When the boat capsized, Diepenbrock fell down the stairs to the engine room, becoming entangled in equipment. Fighting desperately to free himself, he grabbed the legs of a man and pulled himself clear. He swam out of the boat, surfaced, and joined those hanging onto the overturned steamer.[1]

Mel Sparks, sticking to his engineering post as long as possible, was trapped below deck when the boat turned. He worked himself free and swam up close to the steamer. After reaching the *Sea Wing,* he hung on until a piece of wreckage floated by. He abandoned ship and attempted to ride the debris to shore.[2]

Pictured is a close-up of the *Sea Wing's* pilothouse with its distinctive ornate trim. The two men inside resemble Mel Sparks (left) and David Wethern (right).

Captain Wethern was at the wheel when the storm flipped his boat. The pilothouse

Brothers Marion "Mel", left, and Warren Sparks are shown later in life. Mel Sparks, 37 in 1890, co-owned the *Sea Wing* with David Wethern. Warren, 38, worked as a crewman.

door and windows were all closed, trapping him inside. Bracing his feet against the spokes of the ship's wheel, Wethern put his back and shoulders against a window and pushed. The window held firm. Undaunted, Wethern gave a mighty heave, and this time the window gave way. Unable to see in the black water, he swam quickly, hoping his path was across the hull and not along its length. He had to be clear of the ship to surface. After swimming 10 or 15 feet, Wethern was able to rise. Reaching the surface of the storm-tossed lake, he spotted a piece of planking, grabbed onto it, and assessed his situation. He saw the *Sea Wing* floating bottom up, carrying a few survivors who had worked their way onto the flat surface; others floated alongside, maintaining grips on whatever they could find.[3]

Wethern swam to the ship, where crewman Warren Sparks helped him gain a place on its slippery hull. Unable to make out more than shadows of nearby survivors, Wethern shouted questions about the fate of his wife and two children. Though there was no word, the captain's oldest son, 10-year-old Roy, had been pulled to the capsized *Sea Wing* by Andrew Scriber of Trenton. Before the storm struck the steamer, Scriber had donned two life preservers, urging some women passengers to do the same; they only laughed. When Scriber felt the *Sea Wing* roll, he jumped clear and tried to swim away, but the vessel's movements drew him back. He got a handhold on the edge of the ship, and from that spot pulled Roy Wethern to safety. The boy had been in the stateroom when the winds picked up but stepped outside to ask a crewman when they would be free of the heavy buffeting. Standing at the rail in the straw sailor hat his mother had bought, he had been thrown into the water when the ship rolled.[4]

Roy Wethern, oldest son of Captain David Wethern and wife Nellie, was thrown free as the *Sea Wing* capsized.

As he clung to the side of the ship, Scriber realized that those trapped in the cabin were drowning, but there was nothing he could do to help them. With wind, waves and rain still battering the area, neither Scriber nor any of the other survivors on the hull knew how many still clung to the overturned ship. As many as 25 persons, each maintaining his or her position, held on. Almost certainly, the unrelenting storm would reduce their number.[5]

Crewman Harry Niles and Red Wing passenger Robert Chellstrom labored to hold onto the wreckage. Chellstrom's grip, just a fingerhold on a large knothole in the ship's side, was perhaps most precarious. Niles had injured his right hand, but still held firm.[6] The Purdy brothers, Samuel and William, also clutched the ship. Samuel did not reflect on why he had disregarded his premonition of danger just prior to boarding, but focused rather on the horror of what he had just witnessed. Holding tightly to a railing as the *Sea Wing* rolled, Purdy had seen through the steamboat's narrow windows the terrified faces of those trapped in the cabin.[7]

As the shocked and nearly exhausted survivors clung to the overturned *Sea Wing,* the weather took a turn for the worse. Hailstones, some as large as hen's eggs,[8] began to pelt those still on the hull, and they wondered whether they would be able to hold out. Battles for survival continued in the heaving waters. Railroad workers Frank Lampman and Ed Stevens of Minneapolis struggled mightily to keep girlfriends

Annie and Frances Staiger afloat. Neither could swim. Striving to maintain a hold on the women, the escorts attempted to tow them to safety. In desperation, Stevens and Lampman gripped the two sisters by their hair, but the young women slipped from the grasp of the tiring men and disappeared beneath the water.[9]

Frances Staiger

Annie Staiger

Roderic Mero, a 51-year-old farmer from Diamond Bluff, and his 19-year-old son, Austin, both held onto a plank. Strong swimmers, they had a good chance of survival. Alfred Kolberg of Red Wing, another experienced swimmer, headed for the Wisconsin shore. Red Wing resident Oscar Berlin found himself drifting downriver. Also in the water were two 17-year-olds, George Seavers of Red Wing and Robert "Boze" Adams of Lake City. Seavers had jumped overboard when the ship began to roll. He hit the water and was momentarily stunned by a large wave. A flash of lightning revealed some debris floating nearby, and the teenager grabbed a two-foot-wide plank. Adams, separated from friends when he jumped, saw the same piece of wood and made for it, thinking that though he wore a life preserver, the plank would provide extra support. When some life preservers floated by, Seavers donned one and put his arm through the strap of Adams's preserver. The young Lake Citian then hooked an arm through Seavers's preserver. The clear-thinking pair chose not to fight the winds and lake currents, and concentrated on keeping afloat. Hooked together, the two drifted downstream toward Lake City, away from those marooned on the overturned hull of the *Sea Wing*.[10]

People on the barge *Jim Grant* also faced danger. The flatboat drifted away from the *Sea Wing* after the two vessels separated. Nearly 80 people on the barge, almost all men, were still dazed by what had happened. Ed Schenach, the bass fiddler, could not believe what he had just seen: There were more than 100 people on the *Sea Wing*, and he and others on the barge could only watch as they died.[11] The battered *Grant*, meanwhile, had taken

This blurred image of the *Jim Grant*, enlarged from another photograph, is the best available view of that barge. The craft is lashed to the *Sea Wing*, as it was at the time of the July 13, 1890, accident.

on a lot of water but was still seaworthy. Just off Central Point, it was being carried toward land jutting into Lake Pepin.

Lake City youth Harry Mabey, now on the barge, had booked passage on the *Sea Wing* with some of his teenage friends. They first positioned themselves in the cabin, but as the storm neared it filled mostly with women and children. Many in the compartment were praying and crying. Mabey, Boze Adams, Theodore "Theed" Minder and the others abandoned the cabin, donning life preservers as they left. As the *Sea Wing* rolled, the teenagers rushed to the side of the ship and jumped for the barge. One boy crashed through the canopy top of the barge, struck a post, and rolled off. Mabey and Adams missed the barge entirely, falling into the water, but as Mabey surfaced he found himself near the *Jim Grant*. He grabbed its side and pulled himself on board. Mabey hung on as the barge pitched wildly, while winds carried the canopy away.[12]

Charles Lidberg and his friend Oren Oskey, both of Red Wing, had left the *Sea Wing* for the barge before the ship capsized. Now wearing life preservers, they

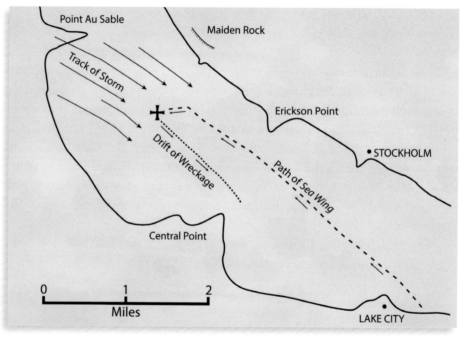

Dr. Thomas A. Hodgson, an expert yachtsman who grew up on Lake Pepin, has studied the *Sea Wing* accident and created this map of the steamer's course.

assessed their chances of jumping off the *Jim Grant* and swimming to safety. Another Red Wing man, George Smith, crossed to the barge, taking a life preserver from under the plank seats, preparing himself for the worst. Fred Scherf, on the barge when the *Sea Wing* capsized, found himself separated from his wife, Mary, and daughter, Harriet "Hattie," who had moved to the ship's cabin. George Reeve, also on the *Grant,* worried for his own safety, but was also fearful for the women, many in voluminous white dresses, he saw struggling in the churning water.[13]

Oren Oskey

Indeed, it became apparent the storm was taking its heaviest toll among the women and young girls. Of the 57 females thought to be aboard the *Sea*

Mary Scherf

Harriet "Hattie" Scherf

Wing when it left Lake City, only a handful could be counted among the survivors. One was Aggie Bartron, on the *Jim Grant* with her fiancé Charlie Truttman. She had heard the orders for women and children to leave the barge for the cabin of the *Sea Wing* but had defied them. Harry Mabey spotted two young women on the barge with a man who had forced them from the boat to the *Grant*, thinking it safer. The women protested, trying to fight their way free, but the man had prevailed.[14]

By now, nearly 10 minutes had passed since the *Sea Wing* turned over, and the survivors' situation seemed to be improving. From their perch on top and alongside of the overturned riverboat, the ship-wrecked began to shout for help. They could no longer see anyone alive in the nearby waters, but lightning occasionally illuminated the white dress of a drowned woman.[15]

Those on the barge faced an important decision. Still adrift, the *Jim Grant* was nearing Central Point. Should the survivors jump off and swim for land or stick with the barge? Harry Mabey knew Lake Pepin well and understood that the waters off the point were comparatively shallow. When the barge struck the peninsula, Mabey yelled to his friends to jump, and he, too, went into the water. About 15 others, including Mabey's pal Theed Minder, also abandoned the barge.[16]

Francis Gartland, a Diamond Bluff railroad depot agent, joined the exodus from the *Jim Grant*, swimming and slogging toward shore, nearing exhaustion. Suddenly, an astonished Gartland witnessed people walking on water. He soon realized the apparitions were survivors wading though the shallows. Charles Lidberg and Oren Oskey went over the side together figuring they could reach land safely, with life preservers providing a bit of extra insurance. Once in the water, however, the two Red Wing friends became separated. Ed Schenach abandoned the barge and was relieved to find his feet touching the lake bottom immediately. The stonecutter waded ashore, but soon found himself in a swamp with water up to his waist. He kept on moving.[17]

Also ready to take their chances in the lake were Charlie Truttman and Aggie Bartron. A strong swimmer, Truttman began towing Aggie to safety. He got her into shallow water and the couple made their way ashore. George Smith, still calm, also left the barge, as did Leo S. Bayrell of Argyle,

Central Point, located at the far eastern border of Goodhue County, is detailed in this 1877 Warner and Foote map. The overturned *Sea Wing* and its barge reached the shallows near the point and came to rest just off its southeast shoreline.

Following the *Sea Wing's* capsizing, its wreckage and the barge *Jim Grant* drifted down Lake Pepin. They went aground separately in shallow water near Central Point, shown here. Wisconsin river bluffs are visible in the background.

Minnesota. He had been visiting his parents in Red Wing and was on the steamer after deciding to take part in the Sunday cruise.[18]

Most on the barge stayed aboard as the *Jim Grant* worked its way off the point, once again drifting free. The hail that had been battering survivors on the overturned *Sea Wing* pummeled the *Grant*. Riders took what cover they could, as those who had left it fought their way to land and safety.

George Smith and a few others now reached shore. They took shelter under some trees as hailstones fell. Harry Mabey crawled into a clump of small bushes, protecting his head with his life preserver. Charles Lidberg, bombarded with egg-sized hail, scrambled ashore without any sign of his friend Oren Oskey. Ed Schenach was still trying to get his bearings. He had found some railroad tracks and followed them to a road. There, he saw a minister driving a buggy and asked for a ride. The minister said the horse already had all he could pull and turned Schenach down. The survivor continued walking.[19]

With the hail diminishing, the worst of the storm was over. For nearly a half-hour the survivors had been punished by straight-line winds, heavy rain and hail. Now, those clinging to the *Sea Wing* and the barge began to hope that those making it to land could get help. On shore, Harry Mabey got to his feet and started the long run to Lake City. As he hurried along, Mabey could still see the barge on the lake. With lightning flashing, he raced to the fire hall and rang the bell. Townspeople responded to the alarm quickly, despite still recovering from the devastating storm themselves.

Within minutes, they were gathering at Oscar Peterson's boatyard to arrange a rescue.

A fearsome challenge faced the citizenry. *Sea Wing* victims needed lifesaving assistance immediately, and the villagers would have to handle the task themselves. National Guardsmen at a devastated Camp Lakeview had yet to learn of the accident. Nearly a half-hour passed before two First Regiment officers riding on horseback reached Lake

A sandy Central Point road, possibly this one shown in 1891, would have been used by *Sea Wing* survivors.
Rest Island and Lake City Souvenir, June 1892

City. They needed medical supplies to treat injured troops. Learning of the *Sea Wing's* peril, the soldiers sent word back to the camp and headed to the accident scene.[20]

Down at the landing, Capt. John S. Howard, owner-operator of the Lake Pepin ferryboat *Ethel Howard,* refused to take his vessel to the disaster site. His new steamer had been making trips between Lake City and the Wisconsin shore for less than

Lake Citian John S. Howard offered this defense of his actions on the night of the disaster. Howard refused to take his steamer, the *Ethel Howard,* shown here, to Central Point in the accident's immediate aftermath.

two months, and though he first agreed to head for the wreck, deteriorating weather changed his mind. Howard already had his ship's steam up when wind changes indicated another storm. He refused to cast off, infuriating some in the crowd. Mayor George Stout and members of the city council offered to guarantee the price of his boat, but Howard would not budge. According to a St. Paul *Pioneer Press* report, the captain asserted, "It is not that, mayor. It is simply that I will add to the number of victims by such an attempt." There was talk of commandeering the *Ethel Howard,* but no one acted.[21]

Survivors still on the overturned *Sea Wing's* bottom ached for help from any quarter—the sooner the better. Residents in the upriver part of Lake City could clearly

WHY HE REFUSED.

Capt. Howard's Reasons for Not Going to the Wreck of the Sea Wing.

Capt. J. S. Howard, of the steamer Ethel Howard, was in St. Paul yesterday. The captain feels very keenly the remarks that have been made about him in the newspapers. His account of the situation last Sunday night is as follows:

I had gone to bed before the storm began, and soon after was called by citizens and went to the boat. Steam was gotten up, and a large number of people were on board who were anxious to go out to the wreck. The wind had veered from the west around to the east, and everything pointed to another furious blow, in which my boat would not have lived a minute. I declined to go out until satisfied that there would be no recurrence of the storm such as had wrecked the Sea Wing. The mayor and members of the council came to me and declared that they would guarantee the price of the boat, to which I replied that I didn't care a cent for the steamer, but did not wish to increase the number of corpses already in the lake, as I certainly should have done had I been caught in gusts such as had been sweeping the lake.

The citizens of Lake City generally feel that Capt. Howard ought not to be blamed for his course, and that his well known courage is a sufficient voucher that he would have faced the storm had he not felt that it would be certain death for all who accompanied him without the possibility of rendering any aid to those already struggling in the waves two miles away.

The Graphic-Sentinel of Lake City, in speaking of Capt. Howard's action, says:

It is due to Capt. Howard to say that the exaggerated stories set in circulation of his unwillingness to go out with his boat after the wreck are foolish and unwarranted. He did go just as soon as he thought it was safe. And our town people may congratulate themselves that they will be safe in the hands of a careful and cautious captain when enjoying a trip on the Ethel Howard. No man has a larger heart or is more ready to respond to the wants of others than he is. If he is cautious when there is danger we are glad of it.

St. Paul *Pioneer Press*, July 17, 1890

This 1867 colorized "bird's eye" view of Lake City features the triangular point that vessels used for docking. The main Washington Street landing area is at the base of the triangle at the image's center, above the small sailboat.

hear their calls for aid. The few clinging to the ship took heart when flickering lights on the pier indicated help on the way.[22]

Then, without warning, the steamboat rolled again, turning from a bottom-up position to its side before coming to a rest. Already exhausted by their battle with the elements, hapless survivors were thrown back into Lake Pepin, among them Captain Wethern. He decided to swim toward shore, hoping to find a skiff and come back for the others. Some grabbed hold of the vessel's now-exposed superstructure.[23]

The ship's new position brought into the survivors' view the bodies of some of the dead in the cabin. One man, clutching doggedly to the ship's railing, saw two women wedged between a stationary seat and the boat's side. Another man saw lightning illuminate the upturned faces of two drowned girls floating by. Yet another spotted the drifting body of a man still wearing a life preserver.[24]

By now, Lake City rescuers were heading toward the shipwreck. Cpl. B. L. Perry, a National Guard Battery B soldier awaiting a train, moved quickly when he heard there were still survivors on the steamer's hull. Upon reaching the lakeshore, he picked out a four-seat rowboat and yelled for someone to join him. Perry considered himself an expert swimmer and knew he could handle oars, but he would need help for the long row to the steamer. Several volunteers stepped forward but, to Perry's frustration, someone in the beach crowd talked them out of joining him. Perry, deciding to go alone, began pushing the boat into the water when Wesley Hills emerged from the crowd. Hills couldn't swim, but he could manage oars. Other volunteers soon manned "a dozen or more rowboats," according to a newspaper reporter, and pulled toward the accident scene. Among those hurrying to the crippled steamer were Fred Foot, Martin Olson, R. L. Terrell, John Foley and H. G. McKinney; also heading out in a boat were accident survivors Harry Mabey and Theed Minder. All those rescuers were from Lake City.[25]

Perry and Hills, quickly on their way, were the first to reach the overturned *Sea Wing*. Initially, they looked to get women survivors into their small craft. Upon reaching the wreckage, the men, according to a Tuesday *Pioneer Press* report, made three trips to Central Point waters, saving 18 women. Perry would later reject the newspaper account with its obvious overstatement of women passengers rescued. He did not, however, detail how many people he and Hills pulled from the water. Nonetheless, the two men acted quickly and heroically, likely bringing several excursionists to safety. In short order, other small boats manned by Lake City civilians were on the scene.[26]

With the last of the survivors off the steamship's hull, rescuers began looking for victims afloat on the lake. The chances of someone still being alive after almost an hour in the heaving waters were remote, but the searchers worked in earnest. Bobbing along well over a mile from the rescuers were Boze Adams and George Seavers, still hooked to each other through their life preservers, drifting farther away from the accident scene by the minute.[27]

In the meantime, others reached safety mostly on their own. Crewman William Sparks had been tossed through the air when the ship turned over. He lost consciousness before being washed ashore several miles downstream, battered but alive. Alfred Kolberg, the Red Wing man swimming toward the Wisconsin shore, made it safely to land at Stockholm, Wisconsin. And stumbling onto the beach near Central Point was the exhausted ship's captain, David Wethern. Edmund Burke, a 20-year-old from Diamond Bluff who had reached land by floating on a plank, saw the pilot struggling and brought him in.[28]

As Wethern gathered his strength, he considered the terrible events of the past hour: the *Sea Wing*, which he owned and piloted, had capsized, drowning perhaps a hundred people; his wife and two young boys were almost certainly among the victims. In no condition to help anyone, he allowed himself to be led to a nearby house.

Chapter 4

"You Haven't Any Little Boy in That Lake!"

To those searching the waters of Lake Pepin, it became clear that their job was no longer one of rescue. Slowly rowing around the area near the overturned *Sea Wing,* they could now only search for the dead. Those first on the scene, with the exception of the First Regiment's Corporal Perry, were all from Lake City. John Berkey, John Hawley and Captain Lewis Lenhart had quickly steamed out to Central Point in a small yacht, saving one person and recovering several bodies. The number of rowboats grew as guardsmen led by Company G's Charles Betcher, Captain of the Guard, and other officers arrived from Camp Lakeview. On the beach, Dr. John C. Adams of Lake City worked feverishly by lantern light, trying to resuscitate the first of the victims recovered from the wreck. The 59-year-old doctor labored without success, in full awareness that his son, Boze, was among the missing.[1]

While some citizens rowed around Central Point looking for the dead, others on shore wondered how to tackle another difficult and unpleasant task—that of boarding the *Sea Wing* to remove the bodies of more victims from the cabin. Those who had been pulled off the overturned boat or who had jumped from the barge and made it to shore were being brought back to Lake City hotels. There, they received dry clothes from storeowners and townspeople before getting some rest. The Purdy brothers were among the survivors reaching Hotel Lyon at 11:30 p.m. There was some other heartening news: The *Jim Grant* had drifted safely to shore on the south side of Central Point and all aboard, now about 60, were safe. They, too, were brought to Lake City for care.[2]

The removal of bodies from the overturned vessel began at midnight.[3] By then the waters

Lyon House (Hotel Lyon), built in 1867, served as a refuge for *Sea Wing* survivors in the hours after the accident. This view is from the 1870s.

The partially submerged *Sea Wing*, shown here with the *Jim Grant* alongside, was in deeper waters when the first bodies were removed from its main cabin. Other steamers later pulled it closer to Central Point.

had calmed, and Capt. John S. Howard's steamer *Ethel Howard* provided a base for operations at the floating wreck. The men going aboard passed bodies up the side of the *Sea Wing* to boatmen who then rowed them to land. Work continued for two hours in the dark, accident victims removed at a steady rate. Locating corpses in the deeper recesses of the cabin was nearly impossible, but at least all the reachable dead had been removed. The rescuers knew others remained, inaccessible until the *Sea Wing* could be righted and brought closer to shore.[4]

Friends Cap Haustein and William Becker, stranded in Lake City after missing the *Sea Wing's* departure, learned of its capsizing. Both had friends and relatives onboard and they ran toward the scene, their path illuminated by flashes of lightning. The pair met an excited young man who shared information about the disaster. The two men moved on, finding the abandoned *Jim Grant*, then recognizing the partially submerged *Sea Wing* out on the lake. Becker and Haustein built a bonfire from wreckage to identify the accident location for those coming to the rescue.

As the fire began to grow, Haustein and Becker noticed a skiff with two men, likely B. L. Perry and Wesley Hills, approaching. The boat held the unconscious form of Haustein's cousin, Annie Staiger. Trying to revive her, the two Red Wing men loosened her clothing and rolled her torso over a nail keg. They could not help her. The boatmen brought two more female victims to shore. Both had drowned. The second was Frances Staiger, Annie's sister.

By 4:00 a.m. the count of bodies pulled from the ship and the water reached 52. Work crews placed the dead near the lake, arranging them in a long row. Located among them was a Bible with the words "May I be prepared to go" written on the

Two men kneeling in the water have apparently found a body in the *Sea Wing's* cabin. The wreckage was still located off Central Point. The St. Paul *Pioneer Press* used a woodblock print, made from this photo, to illustrate their July 15, 1890, edition. They are both shown here.

flyleaf. About an hour later many victims had been loaded aboard, and the *Ethel Howard,* this heartbreaking cargo arranged on deck, started up the river to Red Wing. On board, a correspondent for the *St. Paul Dispatch* dutifully reported the scene. Bodies had been placed in six rows. The first contained the remains of two "young ladies" and two men; the second had seven women, two men, one boy, and a girl; in the third were three women; in the fourth row were nine women, two boys, and a baby; row five contained eight women, five men, and a child; and row six consisted of five women and three boys. The *Dispatch* counted 34 women, nine men, six boys, one girl, and two children—one identified as a baby, the other only as "child"—in the first group of dead.[5]

Red Wing first received word of the disaster around 11:00 p.m. Sunday. Chicago Milwaukee and St. Paul Railroad Superintendent Underwood brought the news when he arrived from Lake City in his private car, which was attached to a

freight train. Chief of Police John Seastrand asked Underwood for a special train. He quickly complied, and a locomotive with cars was on hand within the hour. Carrying several Red Wing citizens, it headed south to the scene of the accident shortly after midnight. The train encountered a freight heading north near Wacouta. It carried *Sea Wing* survivors, including Cap Haustein, William Becker and George Smith. The two trains stopped, with those coming from Red Wing hurrying to see whether their relatives and friends were among the rescued. Some happy reunions ensued.[6]

This view of Lake Pepin looks south towards Frontenac. Steamboats sailing to the northwest past this village brought *Sea Wing* victims to Red Wing.

The trains then went their separate ways, with survivors continuing to Red Wing. Waiting at the depot near the river's edge were over 200 anxious people, also hoping for news of family and friends. Smith, who had been on board the *Jim Grant,* sat answering questions for hours. Some in the crowd followed Haustein, seeking information as he hurried home to change clothes. He wanted to get back to render assistance at the levee.[7]

The *Ethel Howard's* departure provided the work crew at Central Point moments of reflection, but the respite was brief. Workers then laid plans to drag the wrecked

Sea Wing to shallower waters. Now on the scene, Major Arthur P. Pierce, a First Regiment field officer from Red Wing, stationed a military guard a half-mile along the shore on the Lake City side of the point. Torches were placed so that bodies washed ashore could be readily seen by the sentries.[8]

About the time the *Ethel Howard* left Central Point, Dr. John C. Adams, still on duty at the disaster scene, noticed Harry Mabey. That young man had been on board the *Sea Wing* with the doctor's son, Boze, but had no knowledge of his fate. Mabey did report seeing Boze go over the boat's rail in a life preserver. Dr. Adams all but lost hope, telling Mabey that his boy was probably gone. Then, shortly after 5:00 a.m., Boze Adams and George Seavers were noticed walking down the beach. Currents had carried the teens down the lake about a mile past Lake City and then back. They finally drifted near shore at Frontenac, north of the capsized boat. Bystanders helped them to land around 3:00 a.m. They had been in the water for more than six hours.[9]

Adams and Seavers, near exhaustion, looked to Mabey like "washed-out ghosts" as they walked along Central Point. After a reunion with his father, young Adams joined Seavers in a nap on the beach. Later, he told of seeing a woman and child clinging to each other in the water, both in life preservers. Adams soon saw the woman leave the child and sink out of sight. A few moments later the child disappeared.[10]

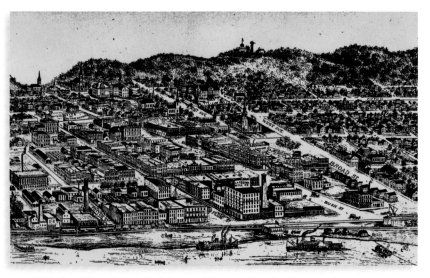

A partial view of Red Wing and its riverfront in 1888 shows steamboats approaching its Plum Street landing. Although the image depicts the levee as empty and open, it typically was cluttered.

The *Ethel Howard* reached the Red Wing levee at 6:10 Monday morning as a large and anxious crowd stood by awaiting word of loved ones. With almost no information about the dead or those who survived, theirs had been a vigil fraught with dread.

To a *St. Paul Dispatch* reporter on board the steamboat, the scene was heartrending. "It was a piteous sight," he wrote, "to see fathers, mothers, husbands, wives, brothers and sisters assembled on the beach as they eagerly scanned the swollen and discolored faces."[11] But, although there was swelling and an occasional cut or bruise, the faces of the dead were calm and peaceful. Only one—that of a woman with eyes wide open, face drawn, and position cramped—showed she had died in agony and fear. The condition of most of the dead, who appeared simply to be sleeping, helped with identification.[12]

Among the bodies were those of Peter and Maria Gerken and four of their five children; there was no word yet of their oldest, Henry.[13] The remains of John Schoeffler, his wife, Kate, and two of his sons also lay on the deck. Searchers discovered Kate while removing victims from the cabin Sunday evening. She clasped her infant son Frederick in her arms. No one had had the heart to separate mother and child, and the two were carried to shore together.[14]

Coroner John E. Kyllo took charge of the bodies, ordering them taken to the undertaking parlors of A. H. Allen on Main Street. Charlie Brown, who owned a local dray line, dispatched teamsters Ole Oskey and Carl Oscar Anderson to the scene with two four-wheeled stoneboats, the beds covered with horse blankets. Usually mounted on runners, the low-slung boats—their flat beds just six to eight inches off the ground—were more often used in quarrying and to remove heavy rock from fields. Oskey and Anderson, assisted by volunteers, moved the bodies onto their vehicles, steeling their own emotions as some in the crowd cried out in grief. The two teamsters knew many of the victims they loaded onto the stoneboats. Ole Oskey's son Oren, a passenger on the *Sea Wing*, was still missing.[15]

John and Kate Schoeffler and their sons John Jr. and Frederick

The horse teams pulled up Plum Street from the levee, turned right, and started down Main Street to the funeral parlor. Relatives joined the grim procession. They would be required to make formal identification. Three undertakers summoned from St. Paul to assist and to bring more coffins and burial robes helped with the process. Soon, the living began their search through the rows of dead, their moans and shrieks nearly continuous; even those without relatives aboard cried in sympathy. Once identified, bodies were removed by families or released to the undertakers for embalming.[16]

Monday's first light at Central Point showed a lake and

Red Wing's Main Street is pictured about 1885, looking toward Barn Bluff. The large building in the distance with five chimneys is the city's Music Hall, located on Plum and Main.

beach littered with chairs, boards, life preservers and other bits of wreckage; the debris strewn for a mile. National Guardsmen, almost all from Red Wing's Company G, worked from eleven o'clock to two or three a.m., rested an hour and were ready to work again. When they saw a body drifting about a hundred yards offshore, guardsman Albert J. Kappel swam out to get it.[17]

Guard officers and local officials worked on a plan to move the wreck close to land to facilitate the recovery of additional bodies. They decided to move the *Jim Grant* near shore and then tow the badly damaged *Sea Wing* next to it so the barge could be used as a base. Corporal Halvorson and a detail of men were assigned the task of towing the barge a mile and a half into position. It would take time, however, to arrange for the move. As work commenced on the wreckage, the crowd at the recovery site grew. Hundreds of people arrived as Lake City residents joined with passengers of an early morning train from Red Wing in seeking word of still-unaccounted-for loved ones.[18]

New arrivals used whatever means of ground transport they could to travel to the wreck at Central Point, and when there were not enough conveyances at the station, some set out on foot. A St. Paul *Pioneer Press* writer drove a team of horses running at a gallop while carrying a party of newspapermen along the beach road. A woman running along the lane dashed in front of the carriage, forcing the correspondent to stop. She yelled that one of the reporters should give her his place in the carriage. Explanations from the men that they were on business did little to impress her. The reporter guided the team around the woman and out into the water. She screamed as they moved past, "You miserable wretches! You haven't any little boy in that lake!"[19]

The magnitude of the disaster became clear immediately to newspaper editors throughout the Upper Midwest. The Associated Press dispatched telegrapher F. A. Presell from St. Paul to Lake City to get news of the accident onto the wire. Presell found the Lake City Western Union office flooded, its windows broken by the storm and wires entangled in the wreckage. Presell began organizing a work crew to build a short line from the wrecked telegraph office to a place where he could tap dispatches to AP members, but he abandoned the effort upon discovering the Western Union lines still worked.[20]

Meanwhile, the search for bodies on the overturned *Sea Wing* continued. Soldiers from Red Wing's Company G, including sergeants Burton Perkins and Oscar Seebach, and privates Abram "Abie" Howe, John M. Olson and Royal W. Hubbell, worked on the ship's hurricane deck. The soldiers, in flannel shirts and uniform trousers rolled to the knees, faced a difficult task. With the ship still on its side, they chopped at the main cabin's roof and broke through in several places. Guardsmen then tore parts of the roofing away, enabling the recovery of bodies that had been out of reach.[21]

One hole made near the pilothouse brought a dress into view. After a momentary silence, one of the men stooped over and pulled on the garment until the body was freed. The guardsman lifted the female victim into his arms, carefully arranged the clothing to cover the legs, and then laid her in a waiting rowboat. He covered the face with part of the ship's flag. The body proved to be that of Bertha Winter, the 13-year-old daughter of John and Dorothea Winter of Red Wing. Before the skiff could move toward shore, searchers discovered the remains of Alice Palmer in the wreckage near the pilothouse. Witnesses theorized that Winter and Palmer were together when the ship capsized; they drowned trying to get out the front cabin door. Guardsmen attached a rope to Palmer's leg and pulled her body, the sixtieth recovered, free. They also found the body of an unidentified man, his foot caught on the cabin ceiling, hanging from that spot. His watch had stopped at 8:30. The remains of Red Wing blacksmith Fred Seavers, whose son George survived with Boze Adams, was recovered at 10:45 a.m. Soldiers pulled the victim through a hole in the deck, then brought him ashore.[22]

Regimental surgeon R. J. Fitzgerald of Minneapolis set up a temporary morgue on the beach with the assistance of Dr. T. C. Clarke of Stillwater and two surgeon recruits from Company G, Elias Magnusson and Bert Clifford. They chose a spot about 50-by-100 feet under a clump of trees, enclosing its boundaries with barbed wire. A fully armed detail of National Guardsmen, under order to keep the crowd from breaking through, patrolled the beachfront morgue. A farmer, his team of horses slowly moving through the sand, brought a wagonload of coffins and pine boxes to the shore, placing the caskets under the trees.[23]

Multiple and varied attempts were made to further the recovery effort. Assuming that many of the missing had sunk to the bottom of the lake, Minnesota National Guard Adjutant General John H. Mullen, now in control of the recovery operation, decided on a unique method of raising them. He ordered the First Regiment's Minneapolis-based Artillery Battery A to cannonade the water. At 11:00 a.m. the

THE LAKE OF DEATH

Its Victims Slumber in the Arms of the Waters That Lured Them to Death.

Others Hear Not the Plaints of Those Who Perform for Them Love's Last Offices

A Voyage of Pleasure That Ended on the Shores of Another World.

The Sea Wing Becomes a Floating Sepulcher for the Pleasure Seekers in Its Cabins.

The Fortunate Few Cling Desperately to the Hull and Face the Storm's Fury.

Death Loosens the Fingers of Many a Weakened Sufferer as the Boat Turns.

Soldiers Forget the Art of War in Their Efforts to Save Their Fellow Men.

Sentinels Pace the Shore and Guard the Watery Resting Place of the Dead.

BENEATH THE WAVES

Another Account of the Awful Fate Which Befell the Excursionists on Lake Pepin.

Weak Women and Children, With Scarcely a Warning in an Unequal Battle Against Death.

Whole Families Forced Into the Darkness of Another World Clasped in Each Other's Arms.

An Awful Sacrifice of Lives as the Wind and Waves Engaged in the Carnival of Death.

Long List of Unfortunates Who Passed From the Sunshine of Life to Death's Shadow.

Sorrowful Scenes as the Friends and Relatives of the Unfortunates Claimed Their Dead.

Red Wing, the Home of Many of the Excursionists, Now a City of Universal Mourning.

Many of the Victims Recovered From the Water and Taken to Their Last Resting Place.

Headlines from the St. Paul *Pioneer Press*, July 14, 1890, provided an overview to the shocking accident.

The Sea Wing Disaster

These photos, taken on the morning after the disaster, show the almost totally submerged *Sea Wing* after the *Luella*, shown in both images, had put the wreckage and the barge, *Jim Grant*, in position for the recovery operation. The difficulty that workers faced in removing the remaining bodies is evident.

The five photos shown here, as well as those on pages 64–65 and 73, are from *The Illustrated American*, August 9, 1890.

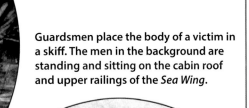

National Guardsmen and civilians had recovered the bodies of 52 *Sea Wing* passengers by 4:00 a.m., July 14. As was the case with the victim shown here, most were found in the steamboat's main cabin.

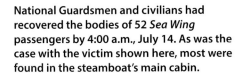

Guardsmen place the body of a victim in a skiff. The men in the background are standing and sitting on the cabin roof and upper railings of the *Sea Wing*.

Bodies were removed from the *Sea Wing* after guardsmen and civilian workers cut holes in the main cabin roof. Most of the victims found in the cabin were female.

unit appeared with two cannon, each drawn by four horses. A rider was positioned on the left lead horse of each unit, and gunners rode along in place. The artillery was unlimbered at the beach, facing the water and the wreck.[24]

Waiting in a semicircle about a hundred yards out on the lake were several skiffs manned by guardsmen. They were to recover bodies raised by the field pieces. Behind the artillery battery the crowd grew silent at the orders to load. At the "Ready" command, some civilians turned away, hunching over. After the order "Fire," the crowd surged forward, some people wading into the water to watch for bodies. Battery A continued its cannonading, but no bodies appeared. Adjutant General Mullen, who was already receiving praise for his aggressive efforts and the manner in which he and his men conducted themselves, ordered the artillery withdrawn, and the unit moved back to Camp Lakeview.[25]

From their preliminary work on the *Sea Wing* wreck, the men knew they would not be able to recover all the dead until decking could be removed and the cabin thoroughly searched. Under direction by guardsmen, Fred A. Young brought his new steam yacht *Wanderer* to the overturned steamboat around noon. A line was attached to the *Wanderer* three different times, but the small craft struggled unsuccessfully to rip the deck away. Next, the *Ethel Howard* tried. Captain Howard threw a line to the men on the wreck and they attached it to the decking. The *Howard* started to move away, pulling the rope tight. Workers heard a cracking sound, then the boat lunged forward, taking with it a piece of the *Sea Wing* deck.[26]

Hope for success increased when a powerful raft-boat, the *Luella,* appeared. Its captain, Antoine Rocque, put himself, his crew and his ship at the disposal of Adjutant General Mullen. With the *Luella* on hand, the *Sea Wing* could be brought to shore and placed next to the *Jim Grant.* Rocque attached a towline to the *Sea Wing* and, after some heavy pulling, succeeded in partially righting it. Then the *Ethel Howard* and *Luella,* flanking the water-soaked wreck on either side, began moving the *Sea Wing.* They were able to drag the hulk no closer than 50 yards from the beach. Resting there, the ship's more normal attitude would facilitate a thorough search of the cabin.[27]

Battery A of the First Regiment, Minnesota National Guard, ordered from Camp Lakeview to Central Point, began the cannonading of Lake Pepin the morning after the accident. They hoped to bring bodies of *Sea Wing* victims to the surface. They are shown here near their Minneapolis headquarters.

Lake City steamboat *Ethel Howard* (background) returns from Red Wing. National Guardsmen, standing in the barge *Jim Grant*, use ropes to keep the *Sea Wing* secure. The steamboat's wheel is visible in the pilothouse, as are holes chopped in the main cabin's roof.

With the steamer righted, workers found three more bodies: Nettie Palmer, whose sister Alice had been found dead earlier; Charles Brown, a 19-year-old Red Wing man; and Henry Gerken, the last of his seven-member family to be located. Gerken, too, had been trapped in the cabin. Mullen and a dozen volunteers then boarded the partially submerged *Sea Wing* to make a final check. The men moved through the cabin shoulder to shoulder in water to their chests, finding no more bodies.[28]

Work continued without interruption, with Adjutant General Mullen sending to Lake City for food and drink for the men. Spectators on shore saw a growing pile of women's hats heaped on top of the barge's small cabin. Some noted the beautiful weather; a bright sun shone, with just a few clouds in a blue sky. Lake Pepin was quiet, impressive in its placid beauty.[29] David Wethern, watching National Guardsmen chop and tear at his once-handsome ship, protested the amount of destruction. Some of the crowd hearing his remarks began to threaten, shouting "Throw him overboard!" and "Send him to look for his passengers!" Alarmed, Mullen advised Wethern to leave the area, and he agreed.[30]

The National Guard soon faced another challenge. No one knew for sure how many passengers were on the *Sea Wing* and *Jim Grant* when they left Lake City, but the best estimate was that over 200 had been onboard. A preliminary listing showed just over a hundred saved and 70 bodies recovered; Mullen knew they still had about 30 more individuals to find.

A dragging operation came next. Work crews tied 500 feet of rope to heavy iron hooks. Manned rowboats, under the direction of Lake Citians Noble Bartlett and William H. McMillan, moved out in a line some 200 yards from shore. They then lowered draglines into the water and began to row slowly toward the beach. Their efforts went unrewarded. Dragging operations continued, now with coiled barbed wire pulled across the bottom of the lake. Once again, workers failed to find accident victims. The frustrated crowd of onlookers turned away in despair. Word spread along the beach, however, that workers would soon attempt to raise bodies with dynamite explosions. The explosive, 150 pounds of it, had already been ordered by telegraph.[31]

One young soldier, working almost nonstop through the evening and into the day, was determined to find his girlfriend. She had been on the *Sea Wing* and was still missing. In the afternoon a note arrived for him. He hurriedly tore it open, read it, and fell to the beach in a faint. She had missed the boat by five minutes and was safe at home.[32]

Meanwhile in Red Wing, city officials assessed the situation, trying to find ways to help. With Mayor Frederick Howe away looking at a job opportunity in Middlesborough, Kentucky, the city council moved ahead on its own. Council member George Cook, on the *Sea Wing* when it capsized, was among those saved. As council president Gustavus A. Carlson waited at the accident site for word of his son, Joe, the other councilmen, John Hack, J. F. Oliva, L. C. Smith and William Hendel, designated him the city's official representative at Central Point.[33]

As the day progressed, there was news of other victims. At 8:00 a.m. a steamer carried eight bodies to Red Wing. At 3:00 that afternoon seven more were brought up from the lake.

At Lake Pepin, John Winter searched for the body of his daughter Bertha. The Red Wing man had driven a horse-drawn carriage to Central Point to conduct his own investigation. He headed for the temporary morgue on the beach without bothering to tie his horse. A guard ordered the Civil War veteran—he wore his Grand Army of the Republic pin—to halt as he neared the barbed wire enclosure. Winter reacted angrily, then asked for his "little girl." The officer in charge could not find her name on his list and informed Winter she must still be in the lake.[34]

The dazed Red Wing man stared down the beach toward a group of young people about a hundred yards away. Thinking his daughter among them, he ran toward them shouting, "There she is!" As Winter drew near, he realized the girl in

On Monday afternoon a group of Lake City men, directed by Noble Bartlett and William H. McMillan, began dragging operations off Central Point. When draglines failed to bring drowning victims to the surface, they switched to using coiled barbed wire. The small steam yacht in the photo is likely the *Wanderer*.

the crowd was not his Bertha. He sank to the sand. But the weary father would not give up. He rose and headed off to talk with an Associated Press reporter who had just obtained the latest list of victims. Winter asked whether Bertha was on the list. She was. John Winter moved away to claim his daughter's body.[35]

Guardsmen who earlier found the remains of Knute Peterson, a 30-year-old Red Wing man to be married on July 21, noted he was wearing a life jacket. Peterson's watch had stopped at 11:50, and it was assumed he kept himself afloat for three hours before drowning. With discoveries such as this, the performance of the life preservers available on the *Sea Wing* and *Jim Grant* came into question.[36]

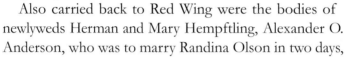

Also carried back to Red Wing were the bodies of newlyweds Herman and Mary Hempftling, Alexander O. Anderson, who was to marry Randina Olson in two days, and Mary Hempftling, aunt of Herman, and her two children, Frederick and Lizzie. William Blaker and Fred Scherf survived the sinking but had suffered heavy family losses. Blaker's wife, Phoebe, and daughter, Cena, had been found dead. Scherf's wife, Mary, and 16-year-old daughter, Hattie, were among the victims taken to Red Wing.

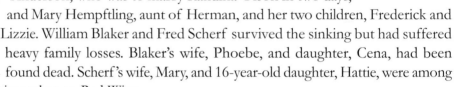

Bertha Winter

Knute Peterson

Dragging operations continued around Central Point throughout Monday afternoon and into the evening. Workers dredged up pieces of fabric from women's dresses, but no bodies. The search on Lake Pepin's surface also continued. Lt. Edwin F. Glenn, an officer of the regular Army, worked with Company G's Charles Betcher in supervising operations later in the day. Others in steam yachts and rowboats crisscrossed Pepin, investigating anything that might be a body. At sunset the National Guardsmen, shortly to resume night patrol of the shoreline, slept while awaiting supper. A detail of cooks worked over campfires to prepare the evening meal. Capt. W. H. Caine of Stillwater, the regiment's cavalry surgeon, was in charge of the evening guard.[37]

In Red Wing, city officials worked on a list of the unaccounted-for. In response to a city council request in local newspapers, citizens came forward with information about the passenger roster. It appeared that 31 persons were missing, with that number expected to rise. Physical descriptions of those yet to be found and the clothes they wore were also collected.[38]

The disaster shocked business activity in Red Wing to a standstill. Normal operations were suspended while recovery of the dead continued. The council ordered saloons closed for three days beginning Monday night. Bodies taken by Coroner Kyllo to the funeral parlor were held for identification, then delivered or released to the relatives, friends or fraternal associations claiming them for burial. The first three funerals took place on Monday evening.[39]

RED WING DAILY REPUBLICAN--EXTRA.

RED WING, MINN., JULY 14, 1890.

A TERRIBLE CATASTROPHE!

THE STEAMER SEA WING CAPSIZED IN LAKE PEPIN.---OVER ONE HUNDRED DROWNED.

NEARLY ALL OF THEM WERE FROM RED WING.

The most terrible catastrophe that has ever occurred in the northwest and one that has few parallels in the whole country happened on Lake Pepin Sunday evening, when the steamboat Sea Wing with all on board was capsized in Lake Pepin, and over one hundred, it is believed, drowned. The majority, in fact, nearly all of these were residents of this city, and the irreparable loss, therefore, comes all the heavier to us. It has cast a gloom over our city that time cannot dispel wholly, for a calamity of this kind can never be forgotten.

The boat Sea Wing and barge, Capt. Wettern commanding, left here about 9 o'clock Sunday morning for Camp Lakeview. The boat had started from Diamond Bluff and in addition to those who boarded here there were a large number from that place and Trenton.

Lake City was reached in safety, the day pleasantly spent there and on the return the party left there about 8 o'clock. Dark clouds drifting about uneasily filled the sky at the time and there were ominous signs that a severe storm was brewing. The captain thought it safe to venture however, and the boat left shore. Everything went well till it had proceeded up the lake a short distance, when the full fury of the storm struck it. It was as nearly as can be ascertained opposite Maiden Rock point. The first severe wind just tipped the boat partially, throwing everybody on to the lower side. Then came a second and stronger gustand the boat was completely capsized. There was no escape for those on board the boat. It turned completely over and was soon filled with water. A few succeeded in getting life preservers, but the great majority were immediately drowned there being no avenue of escape. The overturning of the boat sunk the barge to the water's edge, but it was cut loose from the boat as soon as possible, and after a long time drifted to shore.

It landed about three quarters of a mile above Lake City. As soon as it reached shore some of those on board ran to Lake City and sent boats from there to the rescue of those who were clinging to the capsized steamer. A number of them were so rescued. Word was also sent to Camp Lakeview, and a party was organized, headed by Captains Betcher and Bean, which with lanterns went up the lake shore to search for those who swam ashore and the dead bodies. The steamer Ethel Howard also went out to find the wrecked boat. It was floating near Central Point and work was at once commenced to take the dead bodies from it. By 3 o'clock over fifty had been removed, and the boat then ran up to this city, arriving here at 6 o'clock. The bodies were taken in charge by Coroner Kyllo, and by his orders removed to the undertaking rooms of Swanson & Allen. There a heartbreaking spectacle followed. Wives came searching for husbands, husbands came searching for wives, mothers and fathers looking for children and the anguish was heart breaking in the extreme. As fast as they were identified the bodies were removed to be cared for and others brought in for inspection. Another boat is expected up this afternoon, when perhaps fifty more will be brought to the city.

Following are among those who were saved from the wrecked steamer and barge:

Axel Nelson,
August Olson,
Frank Way, Trenton,
W. Sparks, Trenton,
Oscar Forssell,
C. A. Johnson,
Henry Luft,
W. Boner and son,
G. A. Thompson,
F. C. Lampman,
J. Webb,
John Ammond,
Haskel and Will. Purdy,
Frank Perkins,
Theodore Johnson,
Geo. Cook,
Hugo Herder,
Chas. Fisher,
Andrew Munson,
Geo. Diepenbroeck, Jr.,
Geo. Reeve,
G. Beckmarck,
Claus Saudstrom,
Chas. Lidberg,
Ludwig Rock,
H. Seastraud,
Axel Ekk,
Will Kinney,
Mrs. Hill, daughter and son, Diamond Bluff.
John Kwal,
Edward Axelson,
Otto Simon,
Peter Malm,
Arthur Anderson,
F. P. Gartland,

Oscar Berling,
Robert Shelstrom,
Geo. Hawkins and son,
Jacob Appenceller,
Fred Scherf,
R. F. Johnson,
E. T. Danielson,
W. J., G. and R. Eisenbrand,
Henry Behder,
C. D. Jacobi,
Sherman Ward,
W. W. DeKay, Jr.,
Henry Nelson,
Geo. Lundeck,
A. H. Olson,
N. K. Simmons,
Charles Trutman,
Aggie Bertrom,
May Casey,
Eddie Martinson,
Wm. Ploos,
C. S. Saltzer,
E. D. Morris,
John Nelson,
John G. Gilbertson,
John Anderberg,
G. Larson,
G. Smith,
T. F. Kempe,
E. Schenach,
William Blaker,
The list of the drowned as far as procured is as follows:

Mrs. W. S. Blaker,
Cena Blaker,
Kate Burkardt,
Minnie Fischer,
Annie Snider,
Fred Hottoman,
Anna Way,
Chas. Dinslage,
Kate Dailey,
Phebe Bearson,
C. Johnson,
Geo. W. Nelson,
Flora Smith,
Mrs. F. Hempftling,
Miss Siebrasse,
John Schoefller,
Mrs. John Schoeffler,
Two children of John Schoeffler,
O. A. Anderson, Wilmot, Dak.
Peter Gerken,
Mrs. Peter Gerken,
Peter Gerken's boy,
Lizzie Ann Harrison,
H. Hempftling,
Mrs. H. Hempftling,
Myrtle Mero,
Thos. Leeson,
Pearl Weltern,
Anna Snider,
Emma Nelson,
Mrs. Merritt Green,
Miss Ida Green,
Mrs. Nelson,
Anna Staiger,
Frankie Staiger,
Ida Seavers,
Mabel Holton,

SPECIAL MEETINGS

A special meeting of Red Wing Lodge No. 18, A. O. U. W., will be held this evening.

A. E. Welch Post, G. A. R., will be held this evening.

Colvill Camp No. 33, Sons of Veterans, will be held this evening.

The W. R. C. will meet at their hall this evening.

Lodge No 23, I.O.O.F., meets to-night.

A meeting of the fire department will be held at First ward engine house tonight.

A council meeting will be held at 7 o'clock this evening.

The Red Wing *Daily Republican* rushed out a one-sheet Extra edition on the day after the accident. It contains a list of known survivors and names 38 of the 98 dead.

Chapter 5
Watch for the Dead

Throughout the second night of recovery, the military guard kept spectators off the beach while continuing its watch for the dead. No bodies surfaced, however. With Tuesday's dawn, workers prepared to dynamite the water again. Spectators from the surrounding area began to gather, some still waiting for word of missing loved ones, others curious about the operation.[1]

Dynamiting took place in these waters off Central Point. This photo was taken a year after the wreckage of the *Sea Wing* came to rest there.

John Berkey's steam launch was again pressed into service, this time to serve as a platform for blasting. The lakeshore echoed with the muffled thunder of charges dropped between Central Point on the Minnesota shore and Maiden Rock on the Wisconsin side. Despite 30 dynamite cartridges detonated by Lt. Edwin F. Glenn, no more victims were located. Some believed additional dynamiting to be unnecessary. After additional time in the water, they expected that bodies would become more buoyant and more likely to rise to the surface. Still, the idea of using underwater explosives to raise the dead would not be easily abandoned: delivery of 300 pounds of dynamite was ordered for Wednesday.[2]

Small craft draped from fore to aft with black crepe dotted the lake around the disaster site. Many workers wore badges of crepe or bands of the material around their arms. The majority of men on the work crews, members of Red Wing-based

Company G, continued under the immediate command of Captain Charles A. Betcher. Many searchers had friends and relatives still unaccounted for.[3]

The incessant tolling of church bells in Red Wing on Tuesday morning announced the city's grim task—burial of the dead. At 9:00 the city's three hearses began carrying *Sea Wing* victims to local cemeteries. As the day wore on, makeshift hearses, including express wagons, were pressed into service. The city's three cemeteries were located on the outskirts of town. Oakwood, to the south, had 23 graves waiting on a hilltop overlooking the city. At Calvary Cemetery, two miles south of Oakwood off Zumbrota Road, eight were to be buried. The German Lutheran St. John's Cemetery, west of Red Wing, readied for the bodies of 22.[4]

Present-day photos of Red Wing cemeteries, top to bottom, Calvary, Oakwood and St. John's

Funeral processions filled the streets. The city's business area remained quiet. On Monday evening, stores and shops had opened briefly to supply necessities and the somber clothes of mourning. The idea of a mass funeral for the victims had been dismissed after consideration of time constraints and the difficulty of making detailed arrangements. Families were left to attend to the burial of their dead.[5]

John and Victoria Staiger brought the bodies of their daughters Annie and Frances to their aunt's home on Red Wing's East Seventh Street. The Staigers chose the city house for the wake because they lived out of town on a Florence Township farm. Cap Haustein, a Staiger family nephew, had brought word of the accident on Monday morning, and the Staigers were still reeling from their shocking loss. Haustein traveled by horse cart to the Staiger's house, and also called at the Persig and Hattemer farms to report on *Sea Wing* deaths suffered by those families. Young Mathilda Staiger, seven-year-old sister of Annie and Frances, tried to comfort her parents, but, she recalled sadly, they just "cried and cried."[6]

H. W. Keller of Hay Creek, just south of Red Wing, confronted a daunting dilemma on the day after the accident. His 27-year-old niece, Eliza Jane Crawford, was among the missing *Sea Wing* passengers, and he hesitated to notify her family. Eliza had recently moved to Holden Township in southern Goodhue County where she was teaching. The Ohio native found joy in working with "little Norwegian girls and boys" and wrote home about it. Eliza had been traveling with Katie Burkhard of Hay Creek, whose body was among the first recovered. Clinging to the hope that Eliza might still be alive, Keller decided to wait. He then resolved to head to Lake City and Central Point to assist in the search for bodies.[7]

Mary Leach, back in Red Wing after her ordeal in the storm at Lake City, called on the parents of her friend Minnie Fisher, who had drowned on the *Sea Wing*. Inside the house, she saw Minnie's body lying on two boards, a huge gash across the forehead.[8]

<hr>

While burials continued, rumors concerning the conduct of Captain Wethern and his crew began to circulate. At their heart was the contention that the captain and some of his crew had been drunk when the *Sea Wing* headed back to Red Wing. The charge of drunkenness first surfaced in Lake City on Monday when a Red Wing resident talking with Wethern found fault with the captain's count of passengers on his boat. Wethern, he said, had told him he sold 147 tickets and, with the crew, his family and invited guests, the *Sea Wing* carried a total of around 170. The Red Wing man contended that 187 tickets—not 147—had been sold, and that the number on the ship was over 200. The unnamed man accused the captain and crew of ignorance, incompetence and drunkenness.[9] There was confusion on Monday about the passenger count. The *Daily Republican* reporter heard the captain say he sold about 175 tickets and that the total on board was something over 200.[10]

Reports telling of Wethern's protest about excessive damage to the *Sea Wing* during the recovery of bodies also spread. According to the first rumors, when the captain left the area he crossed to the Wisconsin side of the river with the sheriff of Pierce County, Wisconsin. Later, someone said Wethern was arrested and in jail at the Pierce County seat, Ellsworth, on a warrant sworn out by a friend concerned for his safety.[11]

Perhaps the most serious allegation against the captain was the claim he had ordered women and children into the cabin and then had the door locked.[12] If that was true, those inside the cabin had little chance for survival.

Some of the newspapers, particularly the St. Paul *Pioneer Press*, took the captain to task. A stinging Tuesday editorial, "Man at Fault," opened aggressively: "The worst results of the storm of Sunday are to be set down to the criminal folly of man, instead of being spoken of as the dispensation of Providence." The editors wrote the disaster was "clearly attributable to human recklessness," asserting that Lake Pepin, wide and shallow, was "noted for its ugly seas whenever a storm is on," and no place for an excursion boat during such a tempest. [13]

The editorial described the problems of steamboats on the upper Mississippi, calling them "wholly unfitted" to weather a gale, noting that both their bulk and weight were almost entirely above the waterline: a steamer's smooth keel, light draft and lack of power provided little resistance, while the vessel's bulk presented a large surface to act as wind catcher when exposed to a storm's approach. The writer concluded that the strength of the thunderstorm was spent within a small radius and there would have been no loss of life had nature not been "reinforced by the blind act of its human abettors."[14]

Wethern also had his defenders, particularly Judge Leo S. Bayrell, the Argyle visitor on the *Sea Wing*. The Wednesday *Pioneer Press* quoted his claim that the captain was not only sober, but also in full control of the ship and aware of the danger. Bayrell reported that Wethern walked through the cabin, quietly calming excited passengers, telling them to put on life preservers if they wished. Wethern left the cabin, returning a few minutes later to make the suggestion again.[15]

Bayrell thought the charge of drunkenness stemmed from the condition of some male passengers on the barge who had been drinking

MAN AT FAULT.

The worst results of the storm of Sunday are to be set down to the criminal folly of man, instead of being spoken of as a dispensation of Providence. The deaths at Lake Gervais from a local wind storm, sad as they were, are not to be compared in horror with the tragedy on Lake Pepin. And this latter is clearly attributable to human recklessness, and disregard of the plainest lessons of the past. As to the storm which swept in destructive course past the outskirts of our city, it was the natural outcome of the day that preceded it; such a raging of the elements as follows excessive sultriness, and thermometric and barometric disturbance in every latitude and longitude, without respect to other physical characteristics. The unhappy people who found themselves in its path could not escape its fury. But it was, fortunately, exceedingly limited both in the circle of its action and in the path that it traversed. If no other fatality had marked the day, it would not have been one so black with misfortune for this community. The dreadful disaster was that near Lake City, where some two hundred excursionists were precipitated instantly into a boiling waste of waters, such as inland lakes become under the action of powerful and contrary atmospheric currents. And this portion of the calamity is wholly the fault of man.

It seems incredible still that people should be found to disregard the plain and terrible lessons of the past, in the matter of venturing or remaining upon our inland waters when an approaching storm is in sight. There is hardly one of our picturesque lakes which has not been the scene of some sad accident from exact[,] th[,] s[,] u e. [,] is o[,] f[,] ver[,] n[,]

Two days after the accident, the St Paul *Pioneer Press* placed full blame on Captain Wethern with a scathing editorial.
St. Paul *Pioneer Press*, July 15, 1890

A TERRIBLE CATASTROPHE!

THE STEAMER SEA WING CAPSIZED IN LA[KE] PEPIN---OVER ONE HUNDRED DROWNED.

NEARLY ALL OF THEM WERE FROM RED WING.

THE REAPER

He Gathers a Harvest of Over One Hundred Human Lives on Lake Pepin.

The Terribly Destructive Work of Yesterday's Raging Storm on the Father of Waters.

A Pleasure Party Returning from a Visit to the Militia Camp Swamped by the Waves.

Names of 56 of the Dead Brought to Red Wing Early This Morning---The Suvivors.

DEATH'S PATH.

Lake Pepin Swept by a Cyclone —An Excursion Steamer Swamped.

Over 200 People Struggle for Life in the Middle of the Lake.

The Agonized Shrieks of the Dying Rise Above the Noise of the Tempest.

A Large Number Perish Misab.y, Penned Up in the Cabin.

Others Manage to Clamber on the Upturned Bottom of the Boat.

Those in Comparative Safe Help to Rescue the Less Fortunate.

Parents and Children, Wives a Husbands Locked in Death's Embrace.

A Night of Indescribable Horror —Heroic Attempts at Rescue.

Over Sixty Bodies Recovered as the Result of Untiring Efforts.

Lake City Plunged in Mourning —Heartrending Scenes at the Dock.

A DAY OF FUNERALS.

The Fair City of Red Wing Given Over to Sadness and Tears.

Mournful Processions Wer Their Way Along the Streets.

Many of the Dead Identified ar Removed to Their Last Abode.

NINETY-NINE DEAD.

A List Supplied By the Mayor of Red Wing of Those Who Perished.

The Bodies of All, So Far Reported Missing, Recovered.

There May Be a Few Others, But It Is Scarcely Probable

LAKE PEPIN'S HORROR!

THE FAIR SHORES OF PEPIN THE THEATER OF A DEATH-DEALING STORM!

98 PERSONS FIND A WATERY GRAVE!

and singing as the ship left the Lake City wharf. Their behavior forced some women off the barge and onto the *Sea Wing*. He also supported the captain on the issue of the locked cabin doors, saying Wethern noted the severity of the storm and wished those on the barge to take refuge in the cabin. Bayrell claimed the captain had reconsidered, ordering the women and children onto the *Jim Grant,* though his order was never properly carried out.[16]

The Lake City *Graphic Sentinel* and Red Wing *Daily Republican* led the fight against gossip. The *Graphic Sentinel* reported Wethern was being "severely criticized" for what people were alleging was "criminal carelessness." The paper observed that Lake Citians in the anti-Wethern camp based their charges on the captain's decision to start out in the face of an approaching storm. But the newspaper urged calm, saying authorities in Goodhue County would thoroughly investigate the matter. It advised citizens to "be charitable in our criticisms until the facts come out."[17] It was much the same at the *Daily Republican.* Reporting that Wethern was under fire, the Red Wing paper advised: "Let us be considerate, and at least wait before believing him recklessly imprudent." It urged the public to be "fair in judgment to those who may have erred."[18]

It was quiet Tuesday at Central Point, though the search for *Sea Wing* victims continued. No bodies were found in the morning, but in the late afternoon guardsmen sighted one floating near shore. Sergeant Graw, chief musician of the mounted troop, disclosed it was that of a girl, her remains buoyed up by a piece of wood entangled in her dress. Taken to Central Point and put aboard the *Wanderer* for return to Red Wing, the body was tentatively identified as that of Friedrika "Rikka" Vieths. The *Wanderer,* chartered to serve as long as necessary, set off for Red Wing under the command of owner Fred Young. The ship neared Red Wing about 10:00 p.m., sounding its shrill whistle. People on the street and near the depot ran to the landing for news from the disaster site at Lake Pepin.[19]

As he docked, Young shouted to those gathered that the boat carried a body identified as that of Rikka Vieths. He asked for anyone who knew her to come aboard and verify the identification. The girl's father, Kasper, and two or three others who knew her climbed onto the *Wanderer.* Young removed the cover from the pine coffin, and Kasper Vieths leaned over to

National Guardsmen from Red Wing's Company G, foreground, take a work break during operations around Central Point. Wreckage of the *Sea Wing* is visible in the background.

view the face, now illuminated by a lantern. At first Vieths couldn't make a positive identification, but then he remembered his daughter had been wearing an unusual pair of new shoes. When her feet were uncovered, Vieths identified Rikka. The cover of the coffin was replaced, and the pine box, borne on the shoulders of friends, was taken up the street, followed by the mournful crowd.[20]

Earlier Tuesday evening, shortly after returning from Lake Pepin, Coroner John Kyllo had opened a seven o'clock inquest on the body of North Dakotan Alexander O. Anderson. Perhaps in response to rumors, the coroner ordered a hearing and held it at the undertaking parlors of Arland H. Allen on Red Wing's Main Street. Kyllo summoned as jurors John Nelson, E. T. Howard, Charles Swanson, David M. Neill, William Putnam and John C. Seebach. The group elected as foreman the 42-year-old Putnam, cashier at Pierce Simmons and Company bank.[21]

Rikka Vieths

Constable P. J. Lundquist testified first. The Red Wing official told jurors he had received the body from the *Ethel Howard* on Monday morning. Lundquist removed from the disaster victim a bank receipt, some badly soiled letters, two trunk checks, a watch, two $20 bills and 23 cents in change. Anderson had come from Minneapolis, where he was buying lumber, to spend Sunday with his Red Wing fiancée Randina Olson, still among the missing.[22]

Alexander O. Anderson

At this point Goodhue County Attorney Frank M. Wilson entered the room, asking Kyllo and the jurors who had authorized the inquest. When there was no definitive answer, Wilson directed Kyllo to pick up the copy of county statutes from a table between the corpse and coroner and to read the section about calling a coroner's jury. The reading established that the coroner could not investigate a death caused by accident. Wilson declared there was no legal basis for a coroner's inquest for *Sea Wing* victims. His opinion surprised the jurors and dismayed the anxious crowd gathered near the door.[23]

Juror E. T. Howard asked whether the jury was to be discharged, and Kyllo replied they should consider themselves excused. Wilson then went on to explain his position, saying that action must be based on complaints filed with his office for consideration by the Goodhue County grand jury, which was subject to call at any time. The sideshow ended, frustrating those hoping to get facts about the *Sea Wing* disaster. In the absence of facts, rumors persisted.[24]

The *Pioneer Press* reported a theory advanced by F. J. McIntire, timekeeper for the St. Paul and Duluth Railroad, who claimed to know Wethern "very intimately" but who admittedly had no knowledge of Wethern's condition on Sunday. He said the captain knew the river well, and, "the only way I can explain his starting out upon treacherous Lake Pepin under the circumstances that surrounded him Sunday night is to credit the stories that are told by creditable persons, who say that Capt. Weatheren [sic] was under the influence of stimulants."[25] The story went on to note that reports of drunkenness among the captain and some of the crew "freely circulated, and are not considered improbable by men who know them intimately." The *St. Paul Dispatch* claimed Wethern was intoxicated at the time of the accident and that he reported fewer than the real number of passengers on board.[26]

While things heated up in Red Wing, all was quiet on the lake. Guardsmen maintained their watch throughout Tuesday evening and planned to continue recovery efforts the next morning. Adjutant General Mullen, in overall command since Sunday evening, decided to leave Central Point. He took a train to his home in Wabasha, expecting to return Wednesday.[27]

⌒∾⌒

The picture at Lake Pepin changed drastically during the early morning hours on Wednesday when the lake finally began to give up its dead. Ironically, blasting efforts of the two previous days had nothing to do with the new development. The shal-

This image, from the Wisconsin side of Lake Pepin, shows Point No Point and Frontenac. The building visible is the Lakeside Hotel, a popular resort in the 1870s and 1880s, and a landmark for steamboat travelers.

low, warm water where some of the victims were found had sped decomposition, making them more buoyant. The first bodies, sighted around midnight, floated in a small bay just south of Central Point near where the overturned *Sea Wing* had drifted Monday. Young's steam yacht, *Wanderer,* carried eight of the recovered bodies to Red Wing early Wednesday morning, then headed back for another load. Word around town was that the steamer would return with 16 more dead about noon. As the day wore on, the Red Wing *Advance Sun* reported Lake Pepin "literally dotted with crafts seeking for the bodies which the waters might give up."[28]

A search party of 25 arrived from Red Wing during the night to help. Nineteen of the men were sent by the city council under the direction of Street Commissioner William Llewellyn. Aldermen Hack, Smith, C. E. Friedrich and Oliva had drawn the duty of keeping an official council representative at the scene.[29] Council president and acting mayor G. A. Carlson had led the first crew on the scene. His son, Joe, was still missing.

Identification of the now bloated and blackened bodies was a ghastly task, possible in some cases only through clothing and personal effects. A southern breeze roughened the lake, making work more difficult. Although conditions were not dangerous, only experienced oarsmen were allowed to row the skiffs as the search effort continued. Upon discovery, each body was tied to the back of a skiff, rowed to shore, and maneuvered onto a frame extending into the water. From there the remains were placed in boxes with ice. Sometimes two, or even three bodies were consigned to the same box. The ice, delivered to Central Point by the wagonload, helped retard decomposition.[30]

Slowly, identities of ten of those recovered were confirmed: When the *Sea Wing* rolled, young Willie Jurgensen had been separated from his father, Hans, a Danish immigrant and Diamond Bluff shoemaker. A strong man and good swimmer, Hans reached shore but had been unable to save his son.[31] Lenus Lillyblad, who had earned a free trip by loading ice, was also identified.

The body of 11-year-old Henry Schulenberg joined those of his mother, Sophia, and sister, Minna, recovered earlier. The accident had taken the lives of Christ Schulenberg's wife and three children. Johanna Schulenberg Humpert, older sister of Henry and Minna, was also aboard the *Sea Wing,* and the recently widowed 23-year-old drowned as well. The four family members were buried together in Red Wing.[32]

Ednah Way

John Adams, 19, and Ednah Way, 14, were two of the seven Wisconsin cousins from the Trenton-area Adams and Way families who had been aboard; the bodies of Mamie Adams and Adda Way had been found the first night. Ella and Willie Adams, 14 and 16 respectively, were still missing. Mary Skoglund's corpse had been brought to shore but then taken across Lake Pepin to Stockholm, Wisconsin, where relatives claimed it. Fred Christ and Ira Fulton had gone to Lake City on the *Undine,* and Fulton's prediction of dying like a rat in a trap had proved correct. Their bodies were found Wednesday. The tenth victim identified was 14-year-old Henry Newton.[33]

John Adams

More corpses were discovered as the day wore on. In the early afternoon a skiff brought in the form of a boy about three

Ira Fulton

years old, carried inside the boat rather than towed like the others. No one recognized the swollen corpse. The twenty-first body recovered Wednesday was that of Roderic Mero, a 51-year-old farmer from Diamond Bluff. A nephew and son-in-law identified him. Deep bruises on Mero's head suggested a pounding by the large hailstones. Susan Mero,

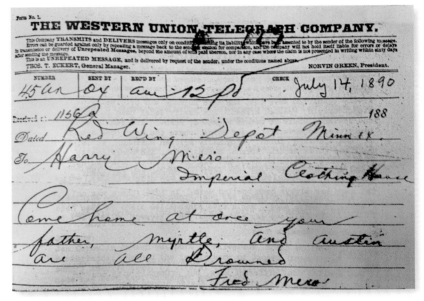

Fred Mero, brother of Susan Mero, sent this telegram to Harry Mero, Roderic's eldest son. It says, "Come home at once your father, Myrtle, and Austin are all Drowned." Roderic and wife Susan were cousins.

Susan Mero

Roderic Mero

Austin Mero

Myrtle Mero

Roderic's wife, had suffered through three days of unrelenting tragedy. Daughter Myrtle, 14, had been found dead on Monday. Lightning from the Sunday storm that took her husband and daughter also struck her barn, killing 11 horses. The family's 19-year-old son, Austin, last seen clinging to the wreckage, was still missing.[34]

Identification of unclaimed corpses proceeded slowly in Red Wing. One body lay unrecognized for several hours until the inscription "Annie, 1882, 8–12," engraved inside a plain gold ring cut from one finger, identified it as that of Peter Olson, 30, of Red Wing. The *St. Paul Dispatch* mistakenly reported Olson's finger had been amputated.[35]

Frank Strope examined a body thought to be that of his son John, 14, finding nothing familiar in the distorted features. He then took a piece of flannel from his pocket and compared it to the shirt on the body. It matched. This, and some familiar shoe buttons, caused Frank Strope's eyes to fill with tears. He had found his son. An unidentifiable body taken from Lake Pepin that day—a young boy with a straw hat still tied to his buttonhole—was the eighty-fifth corpse recovered since operations began Sunday evening.[36]

Lake Pepin yielded little more until a crew member of the steamer *Josie* of the Diamond Jo Line sighted the form of a little girl around 3:00 p.m. The *Josie,* heading up the lake with an excursion party, landed with the body at Central Point. A half-hour later, *Menomonie,* a steamboat from Stillwater-based Branson and Folsom Line, brought in the remains of Austin Mero. The teenager was the third and final victim from the Diamond Bluff family. When the *Menomonie* passed over the site of the disaster, the turbulence it created most likely brought up the remains. G. A. Carlson, directing the rescue operation, chartered the ship for the remainder of the day, asking its captain, Irven Milliron, to steam back and forth in the area.[37]

Dynamiting continued in the afternoon with the detonation of four large cartridges, each containing 50 pounds of dynamite. The work actually complicated the recovery effort; searchers rowed to what they thought might be bodies, only to find dead fish. Despite the confusion caused by ineffective explosives, some remains were located. Rising to the surface, they partially broke through the water. In some instances only hands, pale after being submerged three days, were visible as the bodies floated face up.[38]

By late Wednesday afternoon nearly 30 bodies had been recovered, adding to the mounting death toll, and by 7:00 more had been positively identified, including those of Ella and Willie Adams, a brother and sister from Trenton. Of the seven cousins who boarded the *Sea Wing* in Trenton, only one, Frank Way, survived. Frank's fiancée, Mattie Flynn of Trenton, also drowned. The Adams family had hoped Willie, 16, a crack swimmer who "couldn't be kept down" would be found alive, but his body was located near that of Mattie, whom he had apparently tried to save.[39]

Julia and Anna Persig

William Blaker's loss was complete with the discovery of his son, Delbert. All his young family had drowned. Clothing articles on Julia Persig, 29, also found Wednesday, helped with identification. Her sister Anna's remains had been recovered the first day. The two had been on the *Sea Wing* with their beaus when it capsized. Also located on Wednesday, the day she was to have been married, was the body of Randina Olson. Her fiancé had been the subject of the abortive coroner's inquest.[40]

In the early evening, G. A. Carlson's long wait for his son ended. The thirty-second and last body recovered that day was that of 21-year-old Joe Carlson.

Witnesses who had seen him go over the side of the *Sea Wing* believed he was hit by one of the smokestacks while in the water. The acting mayor, on and off the scene since the accident Sunday evening, remained calm as the corpse was brought ashore. His grief, however, was apparent. Carlson's other son, Theodore, also at the beach, moved quickly into the brush to be alone after he saw Joe's mutilated body.[41]

Even though search teams believed more victims remained in the waters off Central Point, the list of the missing had been reduced and the recovery of bodies was almost complete. The death toll reached nearly a hundred.[42]

Joe Carlson

The remains of Eliza Crawford, the Ohio native teaching in Goodhue County, were also recovered Wednesday morning. While the search for her and other victims continued, Eliza's uncle, H. W. Keller, delayed informing her family of the dire situation. On Tuesday he wrote to her parents about their still missing daughter. After a paragraph describing the terrible accident, his letter took on a personal tone. In his grief, Keller seemed to be speaking for other families with missing loved ones:

> Eliza is among the missing ones & has not yet been found. I was up all last night & today & have not as yet been able to find her. I entertain no hopes whatever of her safety. I have deferred to telegraph you, in hopes that she might be found. She may be found soon & it may be many days yet. We are nearly overcome with grief & fatigue….
>
> There are whole families lost. As far as I know there were only 5 females saved. There were life preservers on the boat but few availed themselves of them…. There is mourning in Red Wing as nearly all were from there….
>
> God only knows the sorrow it has and will cause. We mourn not as those who have no hope. Liza was a good girl & has made many friends in so short a time. You do not know what a painful task this is. Such a disaster has never befallen this country. Poor Frances Jane [Eliza's mother] this will be a hard blow. It is hard for me to write it. May God help you all to bear up is my sincere prayer.

Eliza Crawford

Katie Burkhard, excursion companion of Eliza Crawford

Chapter 6
The Investigation Begins

An official investigation into the *Sea Wing* disaster commenced Wednesday in St. Paul as bodies were still being recovered from Lake Pepin. George B. Knapp and Charles F. Yeager, inspectors from the Galena, Illinois, Steam Vessel District, arrived in St. Paul to conduct the hearings. In the absence of local inspector John Sloan, who was on an official tour of Lake Superior, they worked from Sloan's office in St. Paul.[1]

Knapp and Yeager had stopped to collect evidence at Lake City and Red Wing on their way from Galena. There had been complaints in the two cities about the effectiveness of the *Sea Wing* life preservers, particularly those made of tule reeds (bulrushes). These preservers were divided into twelve sections, each with a 12-inch-long bundle of rushes three inches thick.[2]

This life preserver from the *Sea Wing* is in the collections of the Goodhue County Historical Society in Red Wing.

The life preserver controversy had even reached Washington DC where the Treasury Department was expected to conduct a "thorough inspection throughout the country of all life preservers used on excursion boats of all kinds." Washington had received "unofficial advice" from Minnesota that the *Sea Wing* tule life preservers, when soaked, were "as bad as so much lead," and many of the bodies taken from Lake Pepin were "encased in these soggy bandages."[3]

One critic of the *Sea Wing* life jackets, the unnamed captain of the St. Louis packet *Josephine*, claimed that a captain who would use tule life preservers ought to be sent "to the penitentiary for ninety-nine years," and Wethern should be considered "little less than a murderer." Government regulations sanctioned their use, however, and there were official claims that tule jackets were superior to cork.[4]

Captain Wethern could make a strong case regarding the *Sea Wing's* life preservers. He outfitted his boat with both cork and tule life jackets. The Steamboat Inspection Service in 1887 recommended adjustable life preservers featuring blocks of compressed cork weighing not less than six pounds, although a caveat for preservers of "other suitable material" left room for variety. During the 1880s, at least two California firms were producing approved life preservers made from tule, the kind carried by the *Sea Wing*. Galena inspectors tested a tule preserver taken from the water after many hours of soaking. Tying over 13 pounds of rock to it, they found the preserver could support that dense load in water.

An inscription on the *Sea Wing* life preservers notes United States Inspector Cephas G. Thompson, then Assistant Inspector to Examine Life-Preservers at the Port of New York, approved them for use on July 5, 1887. Investigators also

Discarded life preservers from the *Sea Wing* are visible on the barge. The quality of the life jackets was questioned.

learned Wednesday in St. Paul that the *Sea Wing* had been inspected and certified by the Galena office less than two weeks before the accident.[5]

Capt. David Wethern and six of the *Sea Wing* crew arrived in St. Paul about one o'clock Wednesday afternoon, summoned to testify before inspectors Knapp and Yeager. With Wethern were clerk Ed Niles, ship fireman Henry Hope, deckhands Harry and William Niles and W. W. Willey, and cabin boy Charley Neil, all from Diamond Bluff. They impressed a reporter as intelligent-looking and, with the exception of Wethern and Hope, quite young.[6]

Despite continued allegations of their incompetence and drunkenness, the captain and his crew had been gathering some support. Survivors William Blaker, Hugo Herder and Warren Sparks were quoted in Wednesday's *St. Paul Dispatch:* "We fully exonerate Capt. Wethern from all blame in the lake disaster from which we were saved." Since Blaker lost his wife and two children in the wreck, his words carried extra weight.[7]

Sea Wing co-owner Mel Sparks indignantly denied to newspaper reporters that the captain and crew had been drinking, and said no liquor was sold on the steamer. Sparks also asserted that Wethern had ordered women and children out of the ship's cabin and onto the barge. If those instructions were given—no other witness confirmed them—it is not known if they got through to those in the cabin.[8]

William Blaker lost his family in the *Sea Wing* disaster. Pictured are his wife, Phoebe, and children Cena and Delbert.

The Red Wing *Daily Republican* noted newspapermen from the Twin Cities fomented public anger against Wethern. "The talk of lynching and the like which appears in the city papers," wrote the *Republican's* editor, "is not found here. It exists only in the imagination of the correspondents and should under no circumstances be credited to our people."[9] Nevertheless, stung by the rumors, charges and threats, Wethern and Ed Niles wrote a defense for publication:

> WHAT CAPT. WETHERN SAYS
>
> DIAMOND BLUFF, Wis., July 17–Having heard so many reports of the wreck of the steamer Sea Wing that are incorrect, and thinking that a report from the captain and clerk of the boat, who were on her during it all, would be acceptable to you, we send a report of the trip exactly as it was, as we have seen no report that is exactly correct.
>
> The steamer Sea Wing had been recently inspected and found to be in good condition, and, with the barge she had in company, was allowed 250 passengers. The crew of the boat was:
>
> Captain, D. W. Wethren [sic]; mate, M. L. Sparks; clerk, E. M. Niles; enginner [sic], Will Sparks; fireman, Hank Hope; crew, Will and Harry Niles, West Willie [W. W. Willey], Charles Neal [sic], Warren Sparks.
>
> There were on the boat and barge 200 floats, 187 cork and tule life preservers and 7 good skiffs with 28 oars.
>
> The boat left Diamond Bluff at 7:40 a.m. with 11 passengers, Trenton at 8:30 with 22 more, and Red Wing at 10 with 114 from that point; total, 147 passengers.
>
> As the boat was about to return from Lake City there were two ladies from the steamer Wanderer and eight men from the steamer Undine who wished to take passage to Red Wing on the steamer Sea Wing. These, with about ten more, who were residents of Lake City and who wanted to go to Red Wing, came aboard; thus the list would have been about 175, but some few who came on the excursion failed to get back before the boat left Lake City, hence the number of passengers was under 175. The boat left Lake City at 8 o'clock and proceeded up the lake about five miles. When the storm struck the boat was completely and instantly overturned. Capt. Wethern was at the wheel and did all in his power to keep the boat headed into the wind, and remained in the pilot house until completely submerged, then broke through the side and succeeded in reaching shore. The engineer stood at his post until the water filled the engine room, then made his escape. When the boat upset there was no water in her hull, and nothing but the force of the wind upset her. The barge was not cut loose until the steamer capsized and then only to save it from being swamped also.
>
> The boat was built at Diamond Bluff, was only three years old and was all built new throughout, machinery and all. The boat's tonnage was 109.55 tons. The crew were all able men and understood their business. No liquors were on board and none of the crew drank a drop that day, and more, none of the crew were drinking men. When the boat left Lake City the storm seemed to have passed, and the crew deemed it safe to start. The passengers also wanted to go, and so the boat started out on her return trip. The life preservers were such as the inspector ordered, and were all in good condition. The boat was to start back at 5 o'clock, but most of the number from Red Wing wished to remain until after the dress parade at 7. Hence, the boat delayed until 8 o'clock before starting.
>
> (Signed) D. N. WETHERN Captain. E. M. NILES, Clerk.[10]

Captain Wethern

John S. Howard, the boat owner who had refused to go immediately to the rescue of the *Sea Wing,* was unhappy with the *Pioneer Press* suggestion that his delay had contributed to the number of deaths. The paper ran Howard's account directly underneath that of Wethern and Niles. Captain Howard said he refused to take the *Ethel Howard* out because he didn't believe his boat could survive. When Mayor

Steamer *Ethel Howard*

George Stout and council members promised to guarantee the price of his boat, Howard told reporters he answered that he "didn't care a cent for the steamer, but did not wish to increase the number of corpses already in the lake."[11]

But the fairness of the press wasn't the issue that Wednesday afternoon in the St. Paul office of inspector Sloan. When David Wethern testified before Galena investigators Knapp and Yeager, reporters were not even allowed in the room, despite their vigorous protest that such meetings were open to the public. The captain, as described in a statement obtained later by the newspapers, told Knapp and Yeager that he had been given three issues of pilot's license and two issues of master's license. He also told of being on the steamer full time during the 1888 season and that he had made only a "few short trips" in 1889. He emphasized the seaworthiness of the *Sea Wing*.[12]

Wethern briefly reviewed the Sunday schedule of passenger pickups and went on to a crucial part of his testimony, explaining what he considered the optimum passenger load. "We were allowed 350 passengers with two barges," he said, making one question critical: How many could he safely carry with only one barge? The captain described the safety equipment on board in detail: "We had 175 wood floats, 175 cork and tule life preservers, six axes, seven life boats, and 28 oars." Then he returned to the number of passengers, saying he didn't know how many were on the *Sea Wing;* clerk Ed Niles kept the list.[13]

Departure from Lake City was originally to be after the 4:00 p.m. band concert, according to the captain. "People wanted us to wait until after the 7 o'clock exercises," he said, and to that he had agreed. He flatly denied published claims that a number of passengers asked him not to leave Lake City, and he defended his decision to sail: "I thought the storm was over. No one advised me not to start."[14]

Wethern said he had steamed four or five miles up Lake Pepin, not quite to Maiden Rock. He turned the boat to meet a squall approaching from the Minnesota shore, felt the boat list and ride up again: "We ran that way straight toward the Minnesota shore for several minutes, I couldn't say how long, when a sudden squall came, about straight down the lake, and struck the boat and capsized her instantly." Then he told how he was trapped in the pilothouse and how he escaped, of staying on the *Sea Wing* while it drifted, and how he and the others were washed off when it rolled again, probably from the impact of the cabin or pilothouse striking the lake bottom. He said "nearly all" on the overturned vessel were able to get back onto the wreck. Finally, Wethern told of swimming to shore to get

Passengers board an excursion boat at Lake City's Washington Street landing, about 1900.

a skiff, being too exhausted to return, and someone helping him out of the water. The testimony given by Ed Niles and William Sparks supported his statements.[15]

⁂

At Central Point, officials began to see the end of their gruesome task. With 32 bodies recovered on Wednesday, their analysis showed only one person from Red Wing missing—Rosa Rehder, the 11-year-old daughter of C. H. and Anna Rehder. The body of Rosa's eight-year-old brother, Johann "Henry," had been picked up earlier and buried in St. John's Lutheran Cemetery. Fear that there might be more Diamond Bluff and Trenton victims to be found subsided as the two towns indicated all the Wisconsin dead had been located. Funerals continued in all three communities, though the condition of the bodies recovered on Wednesday and Thursday necessitated immediate burial without regular services.[16]

Diamond Bluff and Trenton, each with ten dead, held funerals throughout the week in the small town cemeteries located near the Mississippi. Trenton residents scheduled a memorial service for local victims a week after the disaster. The observance was held at the town's graveyard, overlooking a back-channel of the river, with speakers including Joseph W. Hancock, a prominent Red Wing pioneer clergyman, the Reverend E. Tucker and M. B. Lewis. Mattie Llewellyn was in charge of music.[17]

Trenton Cemetery is located on a bluff overlooking a Mississippi River back channel. Members of the Way and Adams families are buried here.

In Red Wing, owners draped the fronts "of all the business houses" in black, and door-knobs on the houses of the grieving held funereal crepe. There had been three interments on Monday, 44 on Tuesday, 15 more on Wednesday, and

Diamond Bluff Cemetery includes members of the Wethern, Sparks and Mero families.

nine on Thursday. St. John's Lutheran Cemetery held 33 of the victims, Oakwood 30, and Calvary Cemetery eight.

The city's fraternal and benevolent associations were active throughout the week, helping families of their members arrange funerals. The Odd Fellows attended services for Fred Christ, Ira Fulton, George Nelson, Knute Peterson and Fred Seavers. The Patriarchal Circle also attended the funerals of Christ and Fulton.[18] The Sons of Hermann, a German-American society, were present at the funerals of Christ, John and Dorothea Behrens, and John Schoeffler and his family. The Grand Army of the Republic, A. E. Welch Post 75, attended the funerals of Ella and Mamie Adams, Phoebe Blaker and her two children, Melissa Harrison, Mary Hempftling and her two children, Herman Hempftling and his wife Mary, Oren Oskey and Bertha Winter. Members of the Ancient Order of United Workmen were present at services for the Blakers, Louis Brenn, Fred Christ, Charles Dinslage, George Hartman, the Fred Hempftling family, Lenus Lillyblad and Oren Oskey. The Women's Relief Corps and Sons of Veterans attended the funerals of Christ, Harrison, Oskey, Winter, and the Adams, Blaker and Hempftling families.[19]

There had been offers of assistance for families and individuals who had suffered losses or been rendered destitute by the disaster. Minnesota Governor William Merriam informed *Daily Republican* editor Samuel P. Jennison that St. Paulites had contacted him and stood ready to lend aid. Other unsolicited letters and telegrams flowed into Red Wing offering help.[20]

Red Wing July 22/90

State of Minn
County of Goodhue } SS.

Coroners Report to the Clerk of District Cort of Goodhue County State of Minn regarding the death of Mrs Edd Larson of Red Wing Minne in the disaster on Lake Pepin July 13 AD 1890 and after making investigation I found the following facts

That said Mrs Edd Larson went on the Steamer Sea Wing at Red Wing to go with the excursion party to Lake City and back on the 13th Day of July A.D. 1890 and on her return left Lake City about 8 o Clock said afternoon for Red Wing and after Comming up the Lake about 4 Miles a violent storm arose and capsized the boat leaving said Mrs Edd Larson in the Lake without any Means by which she could save herself from drowning. (above Mrs Larson being 35 years Old)

In the Morning of July 14th AD. 1890 her body was found in Lake Pepin and brought to Red Wing on the Steamer Ethel Howard and left in care of her Husband Edd Larson but he being without Money to pay for Coffin I ordered her to be taken care of by Chas Erikson in the usual manner acording to the direction of the County Commissioners. —

There was no sign on her body of any violence or any reason to believe or suspect any foul play I therefore decided that no inquest was necessary and that she came to her death by drowning from being thrown in to the Lake when the Steamer Capsized on July 13 A D 1890 and so report

J. E. Kyllo
Coroner of Goodhue County
Minn

J. E. KYLLO,
DRUGGIST,

Will always sell you Drugs, Books, Stationery and Wall Paper,
Groceries and Crockery, cheaper than any other
place in the city.

Give him a call and be convinced.
202-204 Cor. Main and Bush Sts., **RED WING, MINN**.

Goodhue County Coroner and Red Wing druggist John Kyllo made hand-written reports, left, for each *Sea Wing* victim. He later transferred the information into the coroner's ledger. There are frequent mistakes in spelling and grammar in these first documents. This entry is for "Mrs. Edd Larson," and details procedures for burial of those unable to afford one. Kyllo's reports and the coroner's ledger are both available for review at the Minnesota Historical Society.

A death certificate specially made for *Sea Wing* victims, below, includes the basic information about the accident in print, with spaces provided for personal details of each victim. This certificate is for a family of three, "Mrs. John Shefler" (Kate Shoeffler) *and* her two sons.

STATE OF MINNESOTA, } ss.
COUNTY OF GOODHUE,

Coroner's report to the Clerk of the District Court of Goodhue County, State of Minesota, regarding the death of *Mrs John Shefler and her 2 children of Red Wing* in the disaster on Lake Pepin July 13, A. D. 1890. After making investigation I found the following facts:

That said *Mr John Shefler with her 2 children* went on the Steamer Sea Wing at *Red Wing* to go with the excursion party to Lake City and back on the 13th day of July, A. D. 1890, and on *their* return left Lake City about 8 o'clock in the afternoon of said day *for Red Wing* and after coming up the Lake about four miles a violent storm arose and capsized the boat leaving said *Mrs Shefler & children* in the Lake without any means by which *they* could save *them self* from drowning. The above *Mrs Shefler* was about *25* years of age. and her *children 6 months Baby and about 2 year old Child in the morning of July 14th* A. D. 1890 *their* bodys was found in Lake Pepin and brought to Red Wing *on Steamer Howard and delivered to Kayser the undertaker for burial*.

There being no sign on *their* bodys of any violence, or any reason to believe or suspect any foul play, I therefore decided that no inquest was necessary and that *they* came to *their* death by drowning, from being thrown into the Lake when the steamer capsized on July 13, A. D. 1890, and so report.

Dated Red Wing, Minn., July 24, 1890.

John E Kyllo
Coroner of Goodhue County, Minn.

M. KAYSER,
MANUFACTURER OF
Caskets, Coffins and Furniture.
722-24 WEST THIRD STREET.

I sell Furniture and Caskets lower than any house in Red Wing, or any city in Goodhue or Pierce counties. My expenses are smaller than any other dealers, for I make my own Furniture and Caskets, and do my own Undertaking and Embalming.

All Work as Good as Done by Anybody in the Business.

Mathias Kayser and his five sons built caskets at their family-owned Red Wing Furniture Company building; bodies were also prepared there for burial.

The strain of dealing with the dead took a toll among the city's undertakers. The first bodies had been taken to Arland Allen's Main Street funeral parlor, but the proprietor, overwhelmed at the magnitude of his task, broke down under the stress. Allen's wife, Anna, contacted Mathias Kayser, owner of Red Wing Furniture Company at 724 West Third Street, asking for assistance. He assumed the job of caring for the dead. Kayser and his five sons worked almost continuously from Monday morning through Thursday, taking care of bodies and building coffins at their factory, breaking only for brief naps.[21]

Despite their remarkable performance during the crisis, the Kaysers found themselves the subject of unfounded rumors. Supposedly, they had taken advantage of suffering families, charging "extortionate prices"—as much as $50 apiece—for handling the bodies in their charge. Mathias Kayser protested the gossip in a letter to the Red Wing *Argus:* "Our charge to those who were able to pay was $5 for caring for the body and $10 for embalming; to those who were unable to pay we charged nothing. The disaster was bad enough as it was, but it was no reason for charging unreasonable prices. For coffins and caskets we did not add an additional price on account of the scarcity."[22]

The services of these men were required in connection with the *Sea Wing* one final time. On Thursday morning a telegram from Lake City Mayor Stout reported the remains of a girl of about 13 had been found. That recovery brought the unofficial death toll to 99. The body was immediately sent to Red Wing on the *Wanderer.*

As expected, the last victim was identified as Rosa Rehder. She was buried next to her brother. Although no one could be absolutely positive, it now appeared all the bodies had been found. Street Commissioner William Llewellyn, in charge of the Red Wing recovery crew at Lake Pepin, called his men to shore. The melancholy search for *Sea Wing* victims had finally concluded. Workers boarded the 12:20 train to return home.[23]

The figure of 99 dead was reduced the next day when Coroner John Kyllo announced that the "Miss Siebrasse," listed in the *Daily Republican* Extra of July 14 and reported as "Kate Sebrass" in the *St. Paul Dispatch* on July 17, was the maiden name of Mrs. Kate Schoeffler, thus counted twice. With the mistake corrected, the victim count from the *Sea Wing* disaster rested at 98.[24]

Red Wing was slowly recovering from its staggering blow. After five days of painful vigil, its citizens had had enough of death. The Red Wing *Daily Republican* reflected the community's emotional fatigue in its Friday issue: "But little remains to be said with reference to the Sunday disaster. The dead have all been buried and business is slowly resuming its normal condition after a period of almost complete paralysis."[25]

This view from 1891, a year after the disaster, looks down Red Wing's Main Street toward Barn Bluff.

Chapter 7
The Awful Pall of Grief

Inspectors Knapp and Yeager reconvened the St. Paul hearing on the *Sea Wing* disaster on Monday, July 21. Members of the Twin Cities press, excluded from the earlier session, had made certain the two inspectors "understood the fact that the public is allowed at such investigations." Wethern, who had told a Red Wing newspaperman he was confident and did not want secrecy, was glad to have reporters on hand.[1]

In the meantime, US Supervising Inspector General of Steam Vessels James A. Dumont, when questioned by the press, admitted all his information came from newspapers and wondered aloud why two inspectors from the Galena district were conducting the inquiry. Unless district boundaries had changed without his knowledge, he said, the case should be under the jurisdiction of the Duluth office. He agreed the hearings should not be secret.[2] In response to the pressure, inspectors Knapp and Yeager issued an order prohibiting any steamer from carrying an excursion party on Lake Pepin unless it was built for "navigating deeper water than the ordinary river boat" and drew at least six feet of water.[3] The inspectors also opened the investigative hearing to the press.

On Monday, Fred A. Young, owner and pilot of the *Wanderer* whose recovery work had been highly praised, testified that he had talked with both Captain Wethern and mate Sparks on the night of the disaster, urging them not to start out from Lake City. A riverman with six years of experience, Young said he asked them to postpone departure for at least an hour, contradicting Wethern's statement that no one had advised him against leaving. Young asserted Wethern also ignored his advice to stay near the Minnesota side of the lake where a couple of wheel turns could bring him to shore. He later saw the *Sea Wing* head for the Minnesota side, but then lost sight of her. He did not immediately go to the aid of Wethern's boat when it rolled because the *Wanderer* was disabled by the wind. In his opinion, Young said, the *Sea Wing* would not have capsized had the *Jim Grant* remained fastened to it. Young did support Wethern on one important point: none of the officers or crew had been intoxicated.[4]

Wethern also received support Tuesday when Capt. James A. Ritchie of St. Paul called him a "skillful master and pilot," cool and self-possessed in the face of danger. Ritchie assailed the character of Fred Young, calling him a liar not to be believed even under oath. Another Wethern supporter, Capt. P. F. Ritchie, praised him as a man of good character and a capable river pilot.[5]

Claus Sandstrom of Red Wing, a *Sea Wing* passenger, told inspectors that although he did not consider it safe for the steamer to start out from Lake City with a storm approaching, he had not heard anyone caution Wethern. Sandstrom, however, acknowledged he had barely reached the boat before it left. Another Red Wing passenger, James Webb, said he thought there were over 200 people aboard the *Sea Wing* at the time of the accident, considerably more than Wethern had indicated. Even so, Webb doubted anything could have been done to avoid the accident: "I don't think the largest boat on the Mississippi could have weathered the gale."[6]

Mel Sparks's testimony about his own qualifications surprised those in the hearing room. He said he served as "acting mate" on the *Sea Wing,* but replied, "No, sir, I do not," when asked whether he held a mate's license. He said he approached Inspector John Sloan shortly before the excursion to inquire about a mate's license and was given the necessary forms to complete. He asked the inspector for permission to act as mate on the July 13 excursion to Lake City, Wethern vouching for his competence. Sloan granted permission after learning that Sparks had worked on the river 12 years and held an engineer's license.[7]

The hearing was postponed after Tuesday's testimony to allow inspectors Knapp, Yeager and Sloan to journey downriver. They hoped to obtain statements from all the surviving passengers of the *Sea Wing* and *Jim Grant.* Such a full account would allow the inspectors to focus in detail on one of the most important questions raised in the hearings: Had the *Sea Wing* carried more passengers than allowed by law?[8]

⋘⋙

While the investigation in St. Paul progressed, leading citizens of Red Wing organized an area-wide memorial service to honor those who had died in the *Sea Wing* disaster. Despite sermons on the tragic event in most of the city's churches Sunday, a special service on a day set apart seemed to be the way to satisfy public need to memorialize victims. Red Wing's city council and board of trade joined forces to arrange for a commemoratory program to be held Friday, July 25, in City Park (present-day Central Park). Charles Betcher, a prominent lumber dealer and father of the Company G commander at Camp Lakeview, was appointed chairman of the joint committee. Jesse McIntire, a Red Wing banker, was named to head the Committee of Reception, a group of 49 prominent businessmen, doctors and city officials. The reception committee at the park was headed by businessman John Rich, and included two councilmen as well as other civic leaders.[9]

Citizens of Red Wing received details about the forthcoming *Sea Wing* memorial service at the "public park" (present-day Central Park). A partial list of committee members is included here.

Mary Sheldon chaired the Ladies Decorating Committee of Ninety-Eight. Theodore B. and Mary Sheldon were perhaps Red Wing's wealthiest and most prominent family and, as a leader in local society, Mrs. Sheldon was the logical choice for the assignment. As with the mens' committees, members of the ladies' decoration group were largely from the city's leading families.[10]

Delegations from many nearby communities were expected to attend. Special trains were ordered to bring Lake City and Rochester mourners to the service. Lake Citians, in particular, were eager to lend support to their neighbors upriver. They had been the first on the accident scene Sunday, many at risk of their own lives. Mayor George Stout and other city officials had spent long hours lending aid and helping supervise, and Lake Citians had been in charge when the last body was recovered. Mayor Stout chaired a town meeting in the Lake City engine house on the Thursday following the accident, at which City Attorney Wesley Kinney introduced a resolution urging the city's common council to assume and pay all just bills resulting from the Lake Citians' rescue and salvage efforts. The resolution recommended that no invoices "be permitted to be forwarded to the city of Red Wing for payment." After debate, the resolution passed.[11]

Working on his own memorial to the victims was James D. Kellogg, owner of a Red Wing photography studio. Advertising each day in the *Daily Republican* for a "picture of the drowned ones," Kellogg hoped to get photographic negatives of all victims to assemble into a composite photograph. He was making excellent progress. *Sea Wing* survivor and bass player Ed Schenach also played a part in providing memorials

James D. Kellogg's Main St. photograph gallery is to the far right.

for the victims. He worked at his full-time trade, stonecutting, chiseling tombstones for the dead. Among the markers he cut was one for the five members of the Hempftling family.

A piece of Ed Schenach's "bass fiddle" is shown. Schenach was a member of the four-piece orchestra hired to play on the *Sea Wing*. This remnant is in the collections of the Goodhue County Historical Society.

In Diamond Bluff there was a bit of good news. Mary Gartland had traveled from New York to claim the body of her son Francis after being notified that he was one of the *Sea Wing* victims.

She arrived to find him alive and well. Her discovery was one of the few happy moments in the midst of long sorrowful days.[12]

Preparations for the Friday memorial service moved smoothly, and all was ready on time. It was a perfect day

This telegram was sent to Mary Gartland announcing the survival of her son, Francis. She had left New York for Diamond Bluff before it arrived.

for the gathering, sunny with an almost cloudless blue sky. A gentle breeze helped cool the air for the program scheduled for 3:00 p.m. Most of the town's businesses were still draped with black and white crepe, and stores and factories closed at noon so citizens could prepare for the observance.

A 20-foot-high obelisk commemorating the *Sea Wing* disaster stands in Red Wing's City Park. Citizens of Lake City prepared the floral tribute "HOPE."

The Sea Wing Disaster

The list of *Sea Wing* victims for whom photographs had been gathered is shown here. Individuals are listed alphabetically, with a photo number that corresponds to that on the composite image to the right.

Adams, Ella–72
Adams, John–83
Adams, Mamie–73, 75
Adams, Willie–74
Anderson, Alexander O.–6
Bearson, Phoebe–57
Behrens, Dorothea–9
Behrens, John–8
Blaker, Cena–41
Blaker, Delbert–87
Blaker, Phoebe–68
Brenn, Louis–45
Brown, Charles D.–42
Burkhard, Katie–76
Carlson, Joseph–90
Christ, Fred–80
Crawford, Eliza J.–65
Dinslage, Charles–86
Fisher, Minnie–63
Flynn, Mattie–18
Fulton, Ira–46
Gerken, Alvina–34
Gerken, Amandus–33
Gerken, Emil–1
Gerken, George–12
Gerken, Henry–29
Gerken, Maria–10, 52
Gerken, Peter–53
Green, Eliza–85
Green, Ida–43
Harrison, Melissa–11
Hartman, George–44
Hattemer, Fred–37
Hempftling, Fred, Jr.–32
Hempftling, Herman–55
Hempftling, Lizzie–30
Hempftling, Mary (Frederick, Sr.)–31
Hempftling, Mary (Herman)–54
Holton, Mabel–48
Horwedel, Theodor–82
Humpert, Johanna–59
Ingebretson, Edward–92
Johnson, Corden–36
Kremer, Millie–89

Larson, Mrs. Ed–25
Leeson, Thomas–77
Lillyblad, Lenus–84
Mero, Austin–49
Mero, Myrtle–50
Mero, Roderic–51
Nelson, Emma C.–66
Nelson, George–16
Nelson, Mary–67
Newton, Henry–23
Niles, Millie–28
Olson, Mary–24
Olson, Peter–47
Olson, Randina–7
O'Shaughnessy, Martin–4
Oskey, Oren–5
Palmer, Alice–56
Palmer, Nettie–20
Persig, Anna–71
Persig, Julia–70
Peterson, Charles–17
Peterson, Knute–22, 81
Rehder, Henry–13
Scherf, Hattie–40
Scherf, Martin–60
Scherf, Mary–39
Schneider, Annie–38
Schoeffler, Frederick–27
Schoeffler, John and Kate–58
Schoeffler, John, Jr.–79
Seavers, Fred–78
Seavers, Ida–26
Skoglund, Mary–64
Smith, Flora–35
Staiger, Annie–62
Staiger, Frances–61
Strope, John–19
Vieths, Friedrika–21
Way, Adda–69
Way, Ednah–88
Wethern, Nellie–2
Wethern, Perley–3
Wilson, James–15
Winter, Bertha–14

Red Wing photographer James D. Kellogg assembled this composite of *Sea Wing* victims' photographs. He said Katie Daily, Leon Kremer and the three Schulenbergs had never been photographed. Neither do John Ingebretson, Willie Jurgensen, Rosa Rehder and Henry Steffenson appear. Mamie Adams, Maria Gerken and Knute Peterson are pictured twice.

The Ladies Decorating Committee of Ninety-Eight had placed impressive floral arrangements throughout the park. Above the north gate was a high arch draped in mourning crepe, and from its center hung a star. Dark pillars were raised on the other three gates, also hung with wreaths and garlands. Trees lining the walk to the speaker's platform in the center of the park were decorated with garlands of flowers. A 20-foot obelisk stood midway between the main entrance and the speaker's stand. It bore 98 diamond-shaped mourning cards, each with the name of one *Sea Wing* victim. The date of the disaster was noted on the back. The cards were intended as remembrances to be taken home by friends or relatives after the service.[13]

Citizens of Lake City added their own floral tribute—a mound of snowy white roses four feet square and about a foot high with a different design at each of the four corners, resting on a unique birch stand. "HOPE," beautifully fashioned from small white flowers and forget-me-nots, graced the front, and "REST" was embedded in dark moss. In the center stood a cross of yellow roses and an anchor of tuberoses nearly two feet tall. The speaker's platform, draped in black and white and decorated with garlands, had a canopy with the words "WE WEEP TOGETHER" made of white flowers on a black background. The front of the stand was festooned with tributes from local societies and individuals. Among the designs were crosses, anchors, pillows, wreaths, and one of heaven's gates ajar. Crosses three and four feet tall were arranged around the park.[14]

Lake City's floral memorial to *Sea Wing* victims

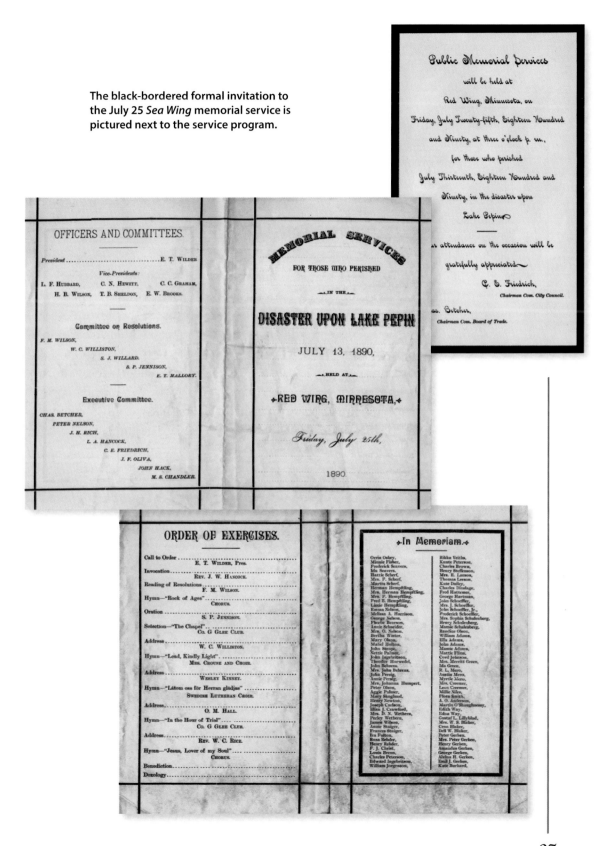

The black-bordered formal invitation to the July 25 *Sea Wing* memorial service is pictured next to the service program.

Friends and members of official committees greeted early trains arriving with visitors from neighboring cities. At two o'clock the bells of the city tolled in unison, a signal for the mourners to gather. Members of social clubs met at various locations in Red Wing, joined other mourners and marched to the park together, entering through a line of National Guardsmen who escorted them to their seats. Soldiers stood in lines along the park's perimeter, while members of the fire department patrolled the grounds.[15]

Shortly after the tolling of bells, special trains from area communities began arriving. One from Lake City carried around 500 people, and another brought 200 residents of Rochester and Zumbrota. Cannon Falls also sent a large delegation. Though Trenton had already held its own memorial program, a sizeable group from that community crossed the Mississippi to attend the Red Wing service. Seats provided for 2,500 filled quickly; additional mourners stood by quietly. The grandstand was packed with speakers, committee members, ministers and officers for the day's proceedings. The women of the decorating committee sat at the rear of the grandstand, joined by the music committee and invited guests. Families of the victims sat at the front near the grandstand. Red Wing newspapers estimated the total number attending the memorial program "conservatively" at 5,000.[16]

The joint preparations committee had asked Judge Eli T. Wilder, a local attorney, former jurist and nationally-known Episcopal churchman, to be the principal speaker, but he had declined, agreeing instead to preside over the service. On the previous Saturday he had been a pallbearer at the funeral of the wife of the Right Reverend Henry B. Whipple, bishop of Minnesota, in Faribault, Minnesota.[17]

After Judge Wilder called the service to order at three o'clock, the Reverend Joseph W. Hancock, first permanent white settler of Red Wing in 1849, delivered the invocation. Goodhue County Attorney Frank Wilson, who had stopped the coroner's inquest, read a resolution of sympathy from Red Wing's board of trade to the mourners. His words expressed the feelings of all: "This city has in deepest gloom, in unutterable sorrow buried its dead, amid the toll of the church bells, the unspeakable grief of the afflicted, the awful pall of grief and mourning that enveloped us all, when our thoughts, all our actions were to relieve the suffering, comfort the broken-hearted and tenderly lay away to rest our dead."[18]

Wilson also read a resolution from Red Wing's city council thanking those who assisted in the rescue and salvage work, naming individuals who deserved special thanks: the captains and crews of the steamers *Luella, Menomonie, Benjamin Hersey* and *Netta Durant;* National Guard Adj. Gen. John Mullen, Capt. Charles A. Betcher and the men of Company G; Mayor George Stout and the men and women of Lake City. The resolution's final words reflected Red Wing's heartfelt thanks to those who had given so much during the tragic mid-July days: "Language is too poor to express the deep sense of gratitude which we feel; and the citizens of Red Wing with one accord heartily join in saying, God bless you for your kind hearts and noble self-sacrificing labors."[19]

Former two-term Minnesota governor Lucius Hubbard, a Red Wing resident, was next on the podium, reading messages of sympathy. A chorus sang "Rock of Ages" preceding the main address by Civil War hero Gen. Samuel Jennison, editor of the *Daily Republican*. Jennison was well-known in Minnesota, having served as private secretary to Governors Alexander Ramsey, William Marshall and Lucius Hubbard. He had previously gained fame when he was seriously wounded while leading the Tenth Minnesota Infantry at Nashville.[20]

City Attorney Wesley Kinney, Lake City

Red Wing attorney William C. Williston, City Attorney Wesley Kinney of Lake City, Red Wing attorney and politician Osee Matson (O. M.) Hall, and the Reverend W. C. Rice followed with shorter speeches. The Company G Glee Club sang two hymns, followed by the Swedish Lutheran Choir. The Reverend J. Wynne Jones of Lake City gave the benediction.[21]

—◦◦◦—

By week's end, steamboat inspectors Sloan, Yeager and Knapp had secured the name of every person known to have been on the *Sea Wing* or *Jim Grant* and finished the formidable task of obtaining affidavits verifying their presence at the time of the disaster. The survivors totaled 103. It would later be discovered that inspectors missed some who lived through the accident. The St. Paul *Pioneer Press* of Saturday, July 26 calculated the total number on board as 203, not including crew, listing 100 dead (98 was the official toll) and 103 survivors. To the newspaper, this settled the question of whether Wethern had overloaded his vessel. The *Pioneer Press* maintained the *Sea Wing*, with only one barge, could carry no more than 175 passengers.[22]

Inspectors returned to St. Paul Monday to hear from David Wethern a second time and to conclude the hearing. Joining them were John Monahan and Michael Chalk of the Duluth Steam Vessel Inspectors Office, who had not been present earlier because of a major sailing regatta in Duluth. Their participation was important because their office had examined the *Sea Wing* before the disaster and pronounced it thoroughly equipped.[23]

> upon ... feet ... of the bridal party
> We are not strangers to your misfortune nor to the scene of its occurrence.
> The disaster, which has left so many vacant places in your homes, caused so many hearts to throb in agony, silenced so many loving voices, dotted your cemeteries with new made graves, and draped your city in mourning, occurred at the gates of our city, at threshold of our homes. In approaching you to-day I realize how unavailing are all human efforts to comfort the heart in an hour like this and in the presence of a sorrow like yours. But, when a sorrow has fallen upon us, when the mind has become weary with reflection, and the eyes dim with weeping, a word of sympathy, however homely or crudely spoken, a tear, while it cannot remove the burden, may, so far as human sympathy can aid those who have been bereft of friends, soften the pangs of sorrow, and assist in preparing the heart to bear the burden, and feeling this to be true we have come to you to-day to express our sorrow for you who are in sorrow, to mourn with you who have been so suddenly called to mourn, and to mingle our tears with yours; and in the name of all the citizens of Lake City, those who are absent as well as those who are present, I extend to you the hand of the sympathy, assuring you that every heart pang you have endured has called from our hearts a responsive throb.
> Spiritual consolation has been and

An excerpt from Kinney's *Sea Wing* memorial service speech reveals the emotion produced by the accident.

Wethern's testimony that day did not bode well for his case. He said he had worked more or less for seven years on the *Mark Bradley* and other boats to learn the

These four photographs from the July 25 memorial service show audience members and the speaker's stand with the words "We Weep Together" arching above.

Several photos taken at the memorial service were stereoscopic; two examples are shown here. The stereoscope was an optical instrument with two eyeglasses that enabled the viewer to look at the two photos at the same time and see image depth.

river but that he hadn't been paid, raising questions about his qualifications for a master's license; furthermore, there was no official record that a master's license had been issued to Wethern. It was evident inspection procedures had been lax.[24]

Boze Adams, the Lake City youth who spent six hours in the water, testified he and several others who had put on life preservers when the *Sea Wing* was only a mile out of Lake City had been reprimanded by one of the boat's officers. "Take that off," Adams quoted the officer, "You will frighten the ladies." Adams described the officer as a man with long whiskers. Asked whether the man was one of two bearded men in the hearing room, Adams replied, "Yes, sir. That's the man," pointing to David Wethern. He added that Wethern's beard had since been trimmed; then he described his ordeal in the water. Wethern was promised an opportunity to rebut Adams's account.[25]

With the conclusion of Monday's testimony, the major part of the investigation was complete and the inspectors faced the task of sifting through the evidence to reach a judgment. It appeared the case of the *Sea Wing* would soon be closed.

As life returned to normal in the small Mississippi River cities that had suffered through the *Sea Wing* ordeal, reporters found Steamboat Inspector General James Dumont a good source of information about the final account of the disaster. He had carefully reviewed the findings of local investigators in St. Paul. Dumont talked freely about the *Sea Wing* hearings when he arrived back in Washington DC on August 18. The inspector general said that although the official report was not yet in his hands, he knew Captain Wethern "would be severely censured for his action in leaving port in the face of the storm and that his license would be revoked."[26]

The Red Wing *Argus* reported on August 21 that Dumont had met in St. Paul with the inspectors in charge of the investigation to decide on the form of their final report. He observed that should Wethern's license be revoked as expected, the captain would "escape well if legal actions are not commenced against him for damage by persons who lost relatives in the disaster." The official report, published August 23 in the St. Paul *Pioneer Press,* confirmed the findings disclosed prematurely by Dumont. It outlined events preceding the disaster, set the number aboard at 10 crew members and about 205 passengers, and established the official death toll at 98.[27]

Themselves river pilots, inspectors George Knapp and Charles Yeager placed the blame for the *Sea Wing* disaster on Capt. David Niles Wethern. At the heart of their decision was their finding that he had violated three sections of the statutes regulating steam vessels, and a good part of a fourth relating to a captain's abilities. The inspectors charged Wethern with "unskillfulness," specifically erring in his decision to start out in the face of an approaching storm and failing to run close to the Minnesota shore where there were good harbors "every mile or so."[28]

Citing a section on overloading—"It shall not be lawful to take on board of any steamer a greater number of passengers than is stated in the certificate of inspection"—the inspectors clearly disputed Wethern's passenger count and disagreed with his judgment that the *Sea Wing* and barge "was allowed 250 passengers." Their estimate of the number aboard, approximately 215 including crew, was "about 30" more than the vessels should have carried. Except for trips under a hundred miles, when the rule was to record only "the number of passengers" aboard, masters of every passenger steamer were directed by regulation to keep an accurate list of the names of all passengers received and delivered from day to day. The inspectors found Wethern had violated this requirement as well, even though the *Sea Wing* trip was under the mileage limit. Duluth inspectors Monahan and Chalk concurred with the conclusions of the St. Paul investigators "without further suggestions."[29]

Finding that the *Sea Wing* "did not have the pilot nor sufficient crew required by her certificate of inspection and permit," Knapp and Yeager ordered Wethern's license suspended and asked US District Attorney Hay to prosecute the captain.[30]

CAPSIZING OF THE STEAMER SEA WING AT LAKE PEPIN

The St. Paul *Daily Globe* of July 15, 1890, shows *Sea Wing* passengers struggling to survive.

The following newspaper article, including the official inspector report of the *Sea Wing* investigation, appeared on the front page of the Red Wing *Advance Sun* on August 27, 1890:

CAPT. WETHERN CENSURED

And His Case Reported to the District Attorney for Prosecution

The full report of the local board of inspectors in the *Sea Wing* disaster has been completed. It is as follows.

Hon. John D. Sloane, Supervising Inspector of Steam Vessels, St. Paul–Sir: We have the honor to state that his board held an investigation on July 16 to determine the cause that led to the capsizing of the steamer *Sea Wing* on Lake Pepin, July 13, 1890. We respectfully submit herewith our decision in the matter, together with a copy of all evidence taken. The evidence shows that the steamer *Sea Wing* was engaged in running an excursion on July 13, 1890, from Diamond Bluff, Wis., to Lake City Minn., and return, and that at the time the Sea Wing left on her return, about 8 o'clock p.m., there was every indication of an approaching storm, although the witnesses in behalf of the steamer claim that it could not be seen from where she lay behind the Lake City point. At the time the *Sea Wing* left Lake City the wind was blowing nearly straight up the lake, but after she had been out thirty or forty minutes the wind suddenly changed and blew off the Minnesota shore. The steamer was then headed directly into the wind and for the Minnesota shore. She had been running in this direction about ten minutes when a sudden squall, or gale, coming down the lake struck and capsized the steamer almost instantly.

The steamer was about four miles up the lake from Lake City, nearly opposite Maiden Rock, about an equal distance from either shore. We are satisfied that nothing could have been done to save the steamer after the squall struck her, as it was so sudden and violent. There was on board the *Sea Wing* at the time about 215 persons, including the crew and officers, ten in number, of which ninety-eight were drowned, an excess of about thirty passengers more than her certificate of inspection and excursion permit allowed her. We also find that said steamer did not have the pilot nor sufficient crew required by her certificate of inspection and permit.

The steamer was in command of Capt. David Wethern, who was also one of her owners. After a careful review of the evidence we find that Capt. Wethern violated sections 4,465, 4,467, Revised Statutes, and so much of section 4,450 as relates to unskillfulness.

Unskillfulness by starting out, as he did, in the face of an approaching storm; also, after he had started out by not running close to the Minnesota shore, "where there are good harbors every mile or so," instead of going up the center of the lake. We, therefore, this day revoke his license as master and pilot, and report the case this day to the United States district attorney for prosecution.

GEORGE B. KNAPP, CHARLES F. YEAGER, Local Inspectors.

The report was sent to Duluth to be reviewed by Inspectors Monahan and Chalk, who replied as follows, under date of Aug. 21:

Hon. John D. Sloane, St. Paul—Dear Sir: This office is in recept [*sic*] of yours of the 20th, inclosing the report and decision of the local inspectors in the *Sea Wing* disaster. We have carefully examined the same, also the evidence, and in our opinion the decision is justifiable, and we concur in the same without further suggestions. Respectfully,

JOHN MONAHAN, MICHAEL F. CHALK.

Chapter 8
Aftermath

The steamboat inspectors' report represented the final official word on the *Sea Wing* disaster. Nonetheless, some questions about the Lake Pepin tragedy will never be answered with certainty. How many excursionists were there? Without a passenger list, we must rely on the inspectors' official report of "about 215," verified by the booklet published in Red Wing in memory of the victims. It lists 213 on board, 156 male and 57 female. Fifty female and 48 male passengers died, leaving 108 male and just seven female survivors. How many passengers were on the barge? This number is harder to determine, but a fair estimate can be made. From the list of 115 known survivors, subtract 25 to 30 survivors hanging onto the steamer's hull, perhaps another 15 to 20 alive in the water, and three who floated or swam to shore to arrive at about 70 passengers on the *Jim Grant*.[1]

Was the barge attached to the steamer at the time it flipped over? Did it matter? Newspapers reported the situation both ways. The Red Wing *Journal* of July 16, 1890, noted that someone said "cut the roper [sic] or we sink," the lines were cut, and a "moment later" the steamer capsized. Two days earlier the St. Paul *Pioneer Press* had reported the barge was cut away, but on July 15 it changed course, asserting the *Jim Grant* had "broken loose." The *Daily Republican* reported on July 14 that the *Sea Wing* nearly sank the barge, which was "cut loose from the boat as soon as possible" after the capsizing. *Advance Sun,* a weekly printed by the publisher of the *Daily Republican,* wrote on July 16 that the "overturning of the boat sunk the barge to the water's edge," the hawser was cut, and the barge drifted away.

Captain Wethern came down on both sides of the issue. He said in 1890, "the barge was not cut loose until the steamer capsized and then only to save it from being swamped also," and then in 1926, the steamer would have escaped "had the barge not been cut loose." Charles Lidberg of Red Wing said the barge was cut

The brief overview found in this memorial booklet provided the only comprehensive look at the *Sea Wing* disaster for nearly 100 years.

free before the *Sea Wing* flipped, but another passenger, George Smith, disagreed vehemently: "So many said that the barge was cut loose before the boat went over, but it wasn't until afterwards. I've had arguments on this point but I wasn't excited and I was right."[2]

Those claiming the barge was cut away or broke loose before the steamboat rolled have gained ascendance over the years, with St. Paul newspapers in 1926, 1930 and 1970, as well as Horace Anderson, Art Saupe and Mathilda Staiger Metzler (relatives of Red Wing passengers), all providing reports agreeing with Lidberg. Certainly, some on board tried to separate the two vessels before the *Sea Wing* rolled. Most reports indicate crew members tried to cut the barge loose, but Saupe asserted a passenger named Eisenbrand (there were three aboard) severed the ropes with an ax.[3] Did the captain order women and children to stay in the cabin or on the barge? Again, reports differ, especially in regard to later instructions given when the squall neared the vessel, and whether or not orders were properly conveyed to the passengers. It is clear that some passengers believed women and children were told to move into the cabin. But was the movement initiated by suggestion, by order, or even rumor? Considering the chaos and near panic as the storm approached, and contradictory accounts in the days and years that followed, it is not possible to determine if Wethern called for the women and children to move to the cabin or to the barge.

Investigators appeared reluctant to attack Wethern's qualifications to run a steamboat, even though questions were raised about his qualification for a master's license and no official record could be found that he actually had one. During a newspaper interview, Captains Charles Meade of Afton and A. R. Young of Stillwater denied Wethern's testimony that they endorsed him for ship's master. In fact, they claimed he was "not competent" for master by "natural aptitude or ability," though Meade had recommended him for a pilot's license.[4]

The investigation also revealed that Mel Sparks, the ship's co-owner, did not have a mate's license. The Diamond Bluff man testified he was the *Sea Wing's* "acting mate" at the time of the accident. Sparks, who held an engineer's license, claimed he had spoken to Inspector Sloan about applying for mate certification and received the necessary paperwork. He asserted Sloan had granted him permission to act as mate. After considering the qualifications of Sparks and Wethern, the steamboat inspectors found the *Sea Wing* did not have "the pilot or sufficient crew" to operate the boat.

In their annual report for 1890, the Steamboat Inspection Service's Board of Supervising Inspectors summarizes the investigation into the capsizing of the steamer *Sea Wing* on Lake Pepin and evaluates David Wethern's actions. It opens with the words "No charges preferred," before noting the captain had been found guilty of violating four sections of the Revised Statues. The summary does mention the revocation of Wethern's license as master and pilot.[5]

An editorial in the St. Paul *Pioneer Press* immediately after Wethern was found guilty of "unskillfullness" reflected the feelings of some regarding the captain:

"Never has sentimentality seemed more wretchedly misplaced than in this instance, where a few people have been heard to express the opinion that Capt. Wethern had already suffered sufficient punishment in his family bereavement and in his feelings. The capsizing of the *Sea Wing* was one of the most appalling calamities in the history of the Northwest. A hundred happy, careless people were hurled suddenly into an awful death. If this event could by any possibility have been foreseen or avoided, then there is no penalty severe enough to be prescribed for those who failed to do their duty."

At best, David Wethern used questionable judgment in taking the *Sea Wing* out in threatening weather and in failing to steer close to the Minnesota shore, but he did not act recklessly, and he did pay dearly for his mistake with the lives of his wife and son. Indeed, this charitable view of the captain seems to have prevailed in

the area, as his position in the community suffered little. A 1909 history of St. Croix County reports Wethern "… is a member of Masonic orders at Red Wing, Minnesota and Prescott," a fraternal relationship indicating his social acceptance in Red Wing. He became active in Diamond Bluff politics, serving as town board chairman for five years and treasurer for two. He later moved to Prescott, Wisconsin, where he shared a home with son Roy. He married Josephine Wheeler of Prescott in 1905.[6]

The captain was interviewed in Prescott by the St. Paul *Pioneer Press*, his most vociferous critic at the time of the accident, for a story in its June 13, 1926, edition. Wethern, 72 years old and retired, said he

David Wethern, pictured in 1926

had completed caulking a boat with Roy in Diamond Bluff the day before the interview: "We couldn't find any good caulkers so I said we'd be damned if we wouldn't do it ourselves."

Wethern died in Prescott at age 75 in April 1929. The funeral was held in the Wethern home, and the captain's body was buried at Diamond Bluff Cemetery. A monument with the names of Wethern's first wife, Nellie, and son Perley makes the plot easy to find. A simple eight-inch stone with the letters "DNW" marks the captain's grave.

These headstones at Diamond Bluff Cemetery mark the Wethern family graves. The inscription for Perley Wethern notes the date of the *Sea Wing* disaster. The stone featuring a dove memorializes their unnamed infant daughter who died shortly after birth. It reads: "We knew thee but a few short hours."

Mel Sparks, along with Wethern co-owner of the *Sea Wing,* died in April 1930 at age 76. His wife, Ellie, one of the handful of women who survived the wreck, had died just four months earlier. Both are buried within 200 feet of the Wetherns. Sparks's brother Warren, who had pulled Captain Wethern onto the overturned *Sea Wing,* lived in Trenton until his death at age 79 in 1931. The other Sparks brother, William, was 62 when he died in 1919. Warren is buried in the Trenton cemetery, and William in Diamond Bluff, next to Mel. The Niles brothers, also crew members on the *Sea Wing,* moved west. Ed, the ship's clerk, became a lawyer in Livingston, Montana, and his younger brother, Harry, joined him there. William Niles moved to Doty, Washington, where he worked in a sawmill.

Wethern's son Roy survived another serious accident shortly after the *Sea Wing* disaster. Young Wethern, according to the Red Wing *Argus,* "nearly blew his hand off" with a pistol eight days subsequent to the wreck, while the hearing was being conducted in St. Paul. In adulthood Roy Wethern would become a well-known and respected Mississippi River pilot. He retired in 1947 to a quiet Highland Park neighborhood in St. Paul. At times he was called back to the river to serve as pilot, and worked part time well into his 70s. He died in 1960 at the age of 80 and was buried near his wife, who died in 1951, and his parents and brother in Diamond Bluff.

David and Nellie Wethern's oldest son, Roy, grew up to be a leading Mississippi River pilot based in St. Paul.

Asked once what effect the sinking of the *Sea Wing* and the loss of his wife and son had had upon his father, Roy noted that Wethern returned to the river despite the accident—"But it was years before I saw him smile again."[7]

The gloomy days of anguish and exhaustion in the communities stricken by the Lake Pepin calamity slowly gave way to the routine demands of life. Newspapers, meanwhile, continued tracking the *Sea Wing* story, publishing related information about the disaster and its aftermath as it came available.

Ten days after the accident, New York Life Insurance agent E. D. Sniffen appeared in Red Wing to pay off two $5,000 insurance policies taken out in May on 22-year-old Fred Christ, son of West Main Street Red Wing brewery owner Jacob Christ. Probate Judge Oscar D. Anderson named William Williston, a Red Wing lawyer who spoke at the *Sea Wing* memorial service, administrator of the Christ estate. Part of the settlement money may have been used to buy the impressive monument that marks Christ's grave in Red Wing's Oakwood Cemetery. Judge Anderson had "a rash of business" at the probate office because of the *Sea Wing* disaster. In the first weeks after the accident, he appointed administrators and scheduled hearings for claims on the estates of eight other victims besides Christ.[8]

By the end of August, photographer James D. Kellogg had in his possession, or had been promised, photos of 93 of the 98 victims. That of Phoebe Bearson was taken

The Christ family marker at Red Wing's Oakwood Cemetery carries the name of Fred Christ.

after her death. According to Kellogg, five victims—Sophia Schulenberg and her two children, Henry and Mina, Leon Kremer, and Katie Daily—were never photographed.

The disaster produced a change in the list of Red Wing's 16 liquor license-holders; four were on the *Sea Wing,* and three—Peter Gerken, Fred Christ and John Schoeffler—died. Schoeffler's establishment was at 302 Main Street, Christ's saloon in West End, 1604 Main Street, and Gerken's at the corner of Fifth and Plum. Fred Scherf, who survived but lost his wife and daughter, oper-ated an establishment at 307 Main Street. Within two months of the accident, the liquor licenses of all four men had been assigned to others.[9]

William Schoeffler's grandparents raised the nine-year-old orphaned by his par-ents' deaths. He passed down the watch found on his father's body to Rod Galvin, husband of his granddaughter Elayne. Gust Lillyblad, whose son Lenus drowned, went back to his grocery and clothing store on Red Wing's Plum Street. Marcella Lillyblad Johnson, a daughter of Lillyblad's second marriage, later lived near Central Point, within a few blocks of the spot where her half-brother's body was found in 1890.[10]

William Putnam, foreman of the halted coroner's jury, was elected mayor of Red Wing later that year, served two terms, and went on to win election, in three successive campaigns, to the Minnesota House of Representatives. Osee M. Hall, a speaker at the memorial service, was endorsed in September by the state Democratic convention for the US House of Representatives. The Red Wing attorney, previously a state senator, was elected in November and served two terms in Congress.[11]

Phoebe Bearson's photo was taken after her death.

An important member of the salvage and body recovery operations went from hero to villain in less than two weeks. Capt. Irven Milliron of the steamer *Menomonie* had refused pay for his work at Central Point, was praised in a Red Wing city council resolution, and lionized at the memorial service. But on July 29, the St. Paul *Pioneer Press* reported that Milliron attempted to kick 17-year-old William Pralow in an encounter in Pepin, Wisconsin. Milliron then drew a revolver and fired at Pralow. The youth dodged, suffering only minor powder burns. Pralow then wrested a picket from Milliron, who had ripped it from a nearby fence, and hit the captain. Milliron tried to swear out a warrant for Pralow's arrest but was, himself, detained.[12]

As acting mayor of Red Wing, G. A. Carlson was delegated by the council to pay unsettled debts resulting from the accident. Among the bills were those for C. E. Hinkley, coffins, $85; steamer *Ethel Howard,* $42.50; Brown's Hotel, meals and lodging, $53.50; Gus Erickson, coffins, $34; and F. A. Young, steamer *Wanderer,* $92.75. Other debts included $13 for extra police at the memorial service; $100 for a Chicago Milwaukee and St. Paul Railroad Company special train; and $87.50 to J. L. Hastings and Son for dynamite. The cost of sending Street Commissioner William Llewellyn and his force to the accident was nearly $1,000.[13]

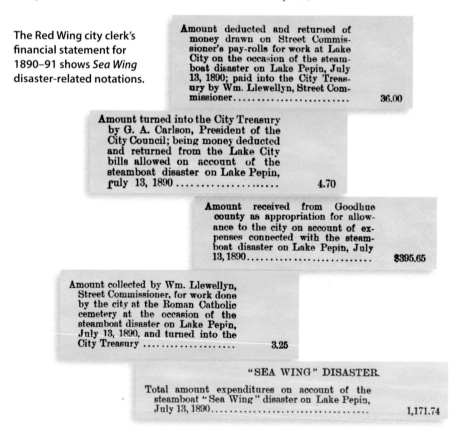

The Red Wing city clerk's financial statement for 1890–91 shows *Sea Wing* disaster-related notations.

Amount deducted and returned of money drawn on Street Commissioner's pay-rolls for work at Lake City on the occasion of the steamboat disaster on Lake Pepin, July 13, 1890; paid into the City Treasury by Wm. Llewellyn, Street Commissioner...................... 36.00

Amount turned into the City Treasury by G. A. Carlson, President of the City Council; being money deducted and returned from the Lake City bills allowed on account of the steamboat disaster on Lake Pepin, July 13, 1890 .... 4.70

Amount received from Goodhue county as appropriation for allowance to the city on account of expenses connected with the steamboat disaster on Lake Pepin, July 13, 1890......................... $395.65

Amount collected by Wm. Llewellyn, Street Commissioner, for work done by the city at the Roman Catholic cemetery at the occasion of the steamboat disaster on Lake Pepin, July 13, 1890, and turned into the City Treasury 3.25

"SEA WING" DISASTER.

Total amount expenditures on account of the steamboat "Sea Wing" disaster on Lake Pepin, July 13, 1890................................... 1,171.74

Carlson had supervised shore operations at Central Point, seeing the bloated bodies as they were recovered, and steeling himself for the sight of his own dead son's corpse. But his wife, Lovisa, alone at home as she awaited word of Joe, had had no such preparation. She insisted on seeing the remains of her son and, upon looking at the swollen, blackened corpse that had been her handsome boy, was shocked into hysterical blindness. Not until surviving son Theodore took Lovisa to her native Sweden on a recuperation trip did she put the horrible image from her mind and recover her sight. Family members remember her husband as "morose and hard to get along with," and Theodore as hard to live with. Theodore's son Robert left home at age 15.[14]

A review of newspaper coverage during the *Sea Wing* disaster and its aftermath finds daily and weekly journals produced mixed results. Some news reports proved objective, and others were occasionally grossly inaccurate. Local papers like the Red Wing *Argus, Journal, Advance Sun* and *Daily Republican* and Lake City's *Graphic Sentinel*, careful in reporting the facts, balanced some of the rumors carried by St. Paul publications. The local newspapers did not devote much space to the human side of the story, however, printing little about the rescue, survivors, salvage or recovery of bodies. Yet, their accurate casualty lists and consistent, matter-of-fact approach had a calming effect on readers. No reports of civil unrest in connection to the disaster surfaced.

Thanks to thorough reporting, the public learned that National Guard officers and men, and families and friends of the victims, did a remarkable job of sorting out problems presented by the disaster. Red Wing's city council acted responsibly and in organized fashion in the absence of the mayor. The only blemish on the city's record is the aborted coroner's inquest on the body of an out-of-state visitor. Examining a corpse could provide little explanation of the disaster, and Red Wing citizens would probably not have allowed one of their own to be displayed in such manner less than 48 hours after the accident. The efforts of Lake Citians, first on the scene, rescuing and recovering more than half the bodies by 2:00 a.m., Monday, were largely overlooked in early newspaper accounts. That omission occurred, most likely, because those civilian volunteers labored in the dark, and National Guardsmen had taken charge by daybreak. As the Lake City *Graphic Sentinel* noted on July 22, "except for two militiamen, all of the work [on Sunday evening] was done by the people of this place and vicinity."

In contrast to the small newspapers, the flowery, flamboyant style of most Twin Cities publications produced lurid headlines like these from the St. Paul *Daily Globe:* "A Voyage of Pleasure that Ended on the Shores of Another World: Its Victims Slumber in the Arms of the Waters that Lured Them to Death," and "The Tornado on Pepin's Treacherous Bosom the Crowning Calamity of All Minnesota Annals." Three St. Paul dailies battled to scoop their rivals, producing some serious mistakes in *Sea Wing* disaster news coverage. Among the most damaging and lasting were allegations that many crew members were drunk. The charges had no merit, but some longtime Red Wing and Lake City residents still believe, incorrectly, the published rumors that Captain Wethern and some of his crewmen were intoxicated at the time of the accident.

St. John's Lutheran Cemetery
Red Wing, Minnesota

1. Gerken: All seven in this family drowned and are buried under this headstone.
2. John & Dorothea Behrens: The Sons of Hermann members, a German-American society, attended the Behrens's funeral.
3. Johann Henry Rehder: He was aboard the *Sea Wing* with his uncle and aunt, Peter and Maria Gerken, and their children.
4. Schulenberg/Humpert: Johanna Schulenberg Humpert, the widowed daughter of Christ and Sophia, was buried with her mother and two siblings, Henry and Minna.
5. Louis Brenn: He was among the last victims to be recovered. This is the family marker.
6. Bertha Winter: Her father, John, searched in vain at Central Point for 13-year-old Bertha.
7–8. Fred Hattemer/Annie Schneider: Fred died on his twenty-fifth birthday and was buried in a grave adjacent to his fiancée, Annie.

Despite such lapses, both the *Dispatch* and *Pioneer Press* had reporters recording in great detail the events at the accident scene, reactions of Red Wing and Lake City residents, and the results of the Wethern hearings in St. Paul. Twin Cities newsmen are credited with forcing the *Sea Wing* hearings to be conducted in public. It is also to their credit that they corrected some of their inaccuracies upon discovery. The coverage of the *Pioneer Press*, even though its early editions had mistakes, was outstanding. Indeed, without the work of the early reporters and their newspapers, the story of the fatal excursion of the *Sea Wing* would have been forever lost.

The *Sea Wing,* though devastated by the July 13 storm and battered by work crews chopping at its decks and pulling at the superstructure, was also a survivor. Two weeks after the accident, the *Netta Durant* steamed to Central Point, attached lines to the wreck's hull and to the barge *Jim Grant,* and towed both back to their home port of Diamond Bluff. Captain David Wethern planned to use the steamer once again.[17]

There is no evidence that a US District Attorney prosecuted Wethern for the "unskillfulness" of which he had been found guilty, and his license to pilot steamers was eventually restored. Wethern continued to run his Diamond Bluff store and keep an interest in vessels working the river. In 1893 he decided to build a new *Sea Wing*, using the hull of the wreck as a base. By December of that year the work was nearly complete, but there was one problem remaining: putting a steamer named *Sea Wing* on the Mississippi could be bad for business.

On December 12, 1893, Wethern asked Pierce County Clerk J. B. Jenson to write a letter to Congressman Nils Haugen of Wisconsin. It read:

> Friend Haugen:
>
> David Wethern of Diamond Bluff this Co. [County] is here, and wants me to write you if possible for you to introduce a bill in Congress, & pass it that will change the name of his Steamboat "Sea Wing" to the name "P.F. Ritchie". You will remember that the Sea Wing met with a sad excident [sic] on Lake Pepin three years ago last July overtaken by a Tornado. Mr. Wethern has raised the wrecked boat and rebuilt her using the hull and other parts of the old in the building of the new boat, and now for various reasons does not wish the boat to have the same name, but not being allowed to change the name without permission from authorities in Washington, which way is troublesome & takes time, so much so that his boat could not receive the new name, before navigation opens in the spring. While by taking this course, the change if allowed, will be made sooner. He says there are no liens or claims against the old "Sea Wing" that would be injured by this change.
>
> Yours truly, J.B. Jenson
>
> P.S. R.S. Rolson can inform you more about this case if necessary
>
> P.S. If old "Grover" [President Cleveland] did not have Congress on his hands, now, we would write to him directly. Wetheran [sic] is one of the sick *Dems* here.[15]

Haugen refused the request because "the rule of Congress is not to grant relief through special legislation where a general law would answer the same purpose," but he visited the Bureau of Navigation on Wethern's behalf. He found that Wethern could secure the change by applying to the collector of customs at the port where the *Sea Wing* was registered.

The *Sea Wing* awaits refitting at Diamond Bluff in the fall of 1893.

Wethern wrote to his congressman, Nils Haugen, hoping to change the name of the rebuilt *Sea Wing*. The request was denied.

Wethern hired owners of the steamer *Netta Durant* to tow the damaged *Sea Wing* to Diamond Bluff.

Wethern did not follow through, and the *Sea Wing* ran on the river under that name for about 12 years until he decommissioned it and sold it for parts. The engine went for his new, larger boat, the *Twin City*, later taken to the southern Mississippi. Salvagers carried away other parts of the superstructure, the hardwood flooring was ripped up, and the gingerbread trim around the pilothouse was used on the front porch of a Diamond Bluff home. Part of the pilothouse was turned into a henhouse, and another section lay near the beach at Diamond Bluff for many years. The original boilers helped power a sawmill near Diamond Bluff until the start of World War II when they were sold for scrap. Two bells from the *Sea Wing*, as well as pieces of Ed Schenach's bass viol, a chair and a life preserver, eventually found their way to the collections of the Goodhue County Historical Society in Red Wing.[16]

For some families and friends of *Sea Wing* victims the tragedy lived on. John Staiger of Florence Township couldn't

David Wethern wrote this message in 1902 using stationery from his Diamond Bluff business. The letterhead notes ties to his new steamer, *Twin City*.

David Wethern replaced the *Sea Wing* with the larger *Twin City* about 1902. He used the engines and shafting of the dismantled *Sea Wing* in the new steamer.

adjust to the loss of his daughters Frances and Annie. His seven-year-old daughter, Mathilda, watched him sit and cry each day after work as he gazed sorrowfully at his daughters' pictures hanging in the family's "best room." Too young to comprehend fully the deaths of her two older sisters at that time, Mathilda, on the eve of her hundredth birthday in 1983, still vividly recalled her mother's reaction to the news. Victoria Staiger stood on the front porch of their farmhouse and "hollered and cried" upon learning of her two daughters' tragic demise. That picture, said Mathilda Staiger Metzler, "is still before me all the time and very clearly."[17]

Anton Scherf of Hay Creek had the watch carried on the *Sea Wing* by his son Martin. After repair, he wore it himself, despite rust stains left on its face by the minute and hour hands. William Blaker put his house in the west end of Red Wing up for sale within days of burying his wife and two children. Sarah Adams of Trenton, who lost three children, two nieces and a nephew, found her striking coal-black hair had turned gray around her face overnight.[18]

Martin O'Shaughnessy of Welch, north of Red Wing, was one of 10 children born to Irish immigrants Tom and Eliza O'Shaughnessy. An anonymous friend of 26-year-old Martin wrote a poem with a sentiment many others mourning loved ones lost on the *Sea Wing* could appreciate:

In the early gathering twilight
Gay and gallant as of yore,
He drove away, and we little thought,
That his last day's work was o'er.
Little dreamed we, that the morrow's sun
Would see him tempest [tost],
And that in the deadly struggle
Death would win, and he be lost.
Was it fate that he should venture,
On that boat doomed to capsize,
He whose only fear was water.
Be pinned so he could not rise?
Oh that fatal, fatal morning,
When he sailed away so brave,
Bent on seeking joy and pleasure,
Doomed to find a watery grave.
Is it right that he be taken,
In his manhood, pride and joy?
Should his mother's heart be breaking.

Martin O'Shaughnessy

Weeping for her noble boy?
Should those restless feet be still
And that voice be hushed and dumb?
He has gone to God in Heaven,
We must say, Thy will be done.[19]

Found at Trenton Cemetery is the marker for *Sea Wing* victims Ella, Willie and Mamie Adams. It is alongside of the newer stone of their parents, Allen and Sarah.

The stone shaft of the Way family marker at Trenton Cemetery is in the form of a tree with its branches chopped away to symbolize life cut short. The small stone topped with a lamb is for the Way boy who died earlier of consumption. It reads, "Our Darling Bennie Gone So Soon."

Two weeks after the disaster, Trenton residents selected storeowner and postmaster Benjamin Way, still in deep mourning over the death of his two daughters, to head a group thanking those who had helped the village's grieving families. "We weep together and the flowers are growing over the graves of our loved ones," they wrote in a short note printed in the commemorative booklet, *In Memory of Those Who Perished in the Disaster to the Steamer Sea Wing on July 13, 1890.*[20]

In death, Benjamin Way's daughters Adda and Ednah joined his third child in Trenton's cemetery; his namesake, Bennie Way, had died from diphtheria in 1882. Way was among the town's wealthiest, most prominent citizens. He held land and timber of his own when he married Ednah Thing in 1863; she possessed extensive real estate. The Ways paid one-twelfth of all taxes collected in Trenton in the late 1880s. But their wealth could not help Way recover from the loss of his daughters. Within a month of the disaster he closed both his store and the Trenton post office, and in late August he sold the building and its stock to C. R. Schact of Hager City. Way retired and died "of consumption" at age 65 in December 1893, his obituary in the *Pierce County Herald* noting that his daughters' drowning was a "shock from which Mr. Way never fully recovered."

Eliza Crawford is buried in Red Wing's Oakwood Cemetery.

Way is buried in the Trenton cemetery under an impressive monument—a 10-foot shaft of stone chiseled in a tree design. Its stone branches are trimmed to symbolize life cut short. A few feet in front of that marker are the graves of Adda and Ednah. Also buried in the Way family plot is *Sea Wing* disaster victim Mattie Flynn, Frank Way's intended bride. Frank, the only member of the Adams-Way family to return from the excursion, died at 91 in 1957 and was interred in the Trenton cemetery.

Christian A. Rasmussen, who worked for the *Daily Republican* at the time of the disaster, observed one effect of the accident in his 1935 history of Goodhue County: "For more than ten years … it was impossible to interest the people of Red Wing and vicinity in any kind of river excursion."[21]

Sea Wing drowning victim Eliza Crawford wrote a letter to her family two months prior to the accident. That missive from the happy young school teacher provided an inadvertent yet fitting epitaph to those lost on July 13, 1890:

"The days fly like moments and I am only sorry to think that too soon these pleasant days will come to a close, as every thing does in this world."[22]

Lake's City's *Sea Wing* memorial marker is on North Lakeshore Drive (US 61/63) between West Green and West Clay streets, on the right when traveling north.

The *Sea Wing* memorial marker is found in Red Wing's Levee Park.

Epilogue

Introduction

The narrow focus of the original *The Sea Wing Disaster* narrative (Red Wing: Goodhue County Historical Society, 1986) did not include extended looks at issues that did not apply directly to the accident. As pointed out in the Author's Note, the first edition, "…considered the events leading up to the disaster, the accident itself, and its aftermath, within a time frame of about three weeks."

The Sea Wing Disaster: Tragedy on Lake Pepin takes a much broader view of the accident, making use of new evidence revealed by extended research and utilizing information produced by others, particularly descendants of *Sea Wing* victims and survivors. The reader should take note that the original version's narrative remains the foundation for the 2014 edition. Additional text has been inserted to amplify or clarify that of the earlier book. Also, any errors found in the first book have been corrected. Endnotes are used to report such mistakes and how they were corrected.

Finally, the limits of the book's structural plan meant that pertinent information of importance and interest would not mesh well if inserted into the narrative. Included in this Epilogue are a number of accounts introduced to assist readers and future analysts in better understanding those terrible days of July 1890.

Cover of the 1986 and 1990 editions of
The Sea Wing Disaster

The Storm That Capsized the *Sea Wing*

In 1990 Dr. Thomas A. Hodgson, meteorologist and principal race officer of the White Bear Yacht Club, analyzed the storm that destroyed the *Sea Wing*. Hodgson possesses another qualification as an accident analyst: He grew up on Lake Pepin and has boated on the lake his entire life.[1]

Hodgson theorizes the storm that swept toward the *Sea Wing* was probably part of a large squall line leading a cold front across Minnesota. Such prefrontal thunderstorms, he writes, typically exhibit the following behavior:

1. Onset of the storm—a gust front of 50–80 mph winds
2. The first third of the storm—heavy rain and hail; sustained high winds
3. The middle third of the storm—heavy lightning, moderate wind and moderate to heavy rain; chance of hail diminishes
4. The final third of the storm—reduced rain, wind and lightning; greatest chance of tornado formation

The tempest that struck the *Sea Wing* generally followed this prefrontal thunderstorm pattern. Hodgson believes straight-line winds and high seas on Lake Pepin capsized the steamboat. Ensuing heavy rain, lightning and hail then assailed the survivors. He attributes the erroneous reports of a tornado at the accident scene to the "characteristic rolling, boiling clouds of the squall line."

Eyewitnesses support Hodgson's contention. Those on the ship's detached barge, *Jim Grant*, reported that two heavy gusts of wind brought about the accident. The first burst caused the steamboat to lurch to starboard, exposing part of its flat bottom; a second gust forced the boat to roll. A tornado did *not* strike the *Sea Wing*, although some witnesses claimed to have seen a funnel cloud in the area.

The study notes the thunderstorm that advanced toward Lake Pepin in July 1890 followed a path over the lowest ground on the Minnesota shore. The part of the squall line that capsized the *Sea Wing*, he theorizes, "…probably moved onto the water between Frontenac and the bluffs south of Lake City." Since wind follows the path of least resistance, Hodgson also believes, "…it is likely that the storm followed the lake's contours, traveling Pepin's length as if held between the Minnesota and Wisconsin bluffs."

Central Point, Rest Island and the Location of the Wreckage

According to *Sea Wing* captain David Wethern and accident investigators, the steamboat capsized in heavy winds and waves some six miles from Lake City. There is agreement that after it rolled, the stricken vessel floated downriver before coming to rest off Central Point. Confusion has arisen, however, in defining the term "Central Point." In the days following the disaster, some accounts reported the wreckage to be in waters near Rest Island. They apparently believed the words "Central Point"

This present-day photo taken from the Rest Island site, Hok-Si-La Park, shows the tip of the Central Point peninsula.

and "Rest Island" could be used interchangeably. Since the location of the *Sea Wing's* wreckage is crucial to its story, clarification is required.[2]

In 1890 the words "Central Point," in the lexicon of Lake Pepin, referred to an eye-catching peninsular promontory jutting into the lake *and* to a township of the same name in which this arm of land was found. Complicating Central Point matters further is the boundary running between Goodhue and Wabasha counties. It places Lake City in both counties, with Central Point located on the Goodhue County side of the divide. The odd-sized Central Point parcel, holding nearly 200 acres and a considerable amount of shoreline, is located in Goodhue County.

Also in 1890, Twin Cities-based anti-alcohol activists were in the process of creating a "refuge for inebriates" in portions of Central Point's sections 30, 31 and 32 that they called Rest Island. It is helpful to remember that Rest Island was *not* an island at all, but simply a name the Twin Cities prohibitionists used for their new Central Point campus. Confusion over the distinction between the Rest Island location (present-day Hok-Si-La Park) and Central Point is understandable since they are adjacent.

Credit Due to Lake Citians was Misplaced

The heroic well-publicized efforts of St. Paul soldier B. L. Perry who, with Wesley Hills, bravely rowed through the storm to the accident scene produced a mistaken impression that National Guardsmen were the first to assist *Sea Wing* survivors at Central Point. While the Guard later proved effective and aggressive in attempting to recover the *Sea Wing's* dead, the Minnesota National Guard (MNG) did not save anyone from drowning. Perry had departed Camp Lakeview and was in Lake City awaiting a train when dangerous winds struck the area. He immediately rushed to the Washington Street landing and soon enlisted the civilian, Hills, to join him in rowing a boat to the wreckage.

No other Guardsmen found themselves in a position to assist *Sea Wing* victims. Straight-line winds that devastated the *Sea Wing* also tore up Lake City and pounded Camp Lakeview. That tent city was virtually leveled. Of the 65 tents pitched on the campgrounds, only five remained standing. Soaked to the skin, soldiers headed to the stables for shelter. With the hospital destroyed by the tempest, MNG regimental cavalry surgeon W. H. Caine and another officer ordered horses saddled and then rode to Lake City. Upon reaching town, they learned of the *Sea Wing's* peril. The two officers ordered supplies to be sent to Camp Lakeview and then headed to the accident scene.

It is clear that soldiers at Lakeview were in no position to offer immediate aid to any survivors at Central Point. Before taking such action, officers and men had to wait for the storm to subside. They then conducted a survey of their camp and the damage sustained. By the time Caine had saddled up and ridden to Lake City, a half-hour had likely passed. Caine took the time to secure and send off "a supply of stimulants"—likely coffee and tea—for the men at Camp Lakeview before riding to Central Point where he would assist survivors. Assuming Caine immediately sent word of the disaster to camp, another half-hour or more would have been used in getting guardsmen moving toward the accident locale.

The MNG report does not mention the time it took to get its men on the scene—90 minutes would seem a quick response—but it does note that, upon arrival, their work was "of rescuing the dead." Thus, with the exception of Perry, those braving Lake Pepin's still very dangerous waters to rescue *Sea Wing* victims were Lake City civilians.

Compelling Testimony

James Webb offered compelling testimony during the St. Paul hearings on the *Sea Wing* disaster. The information he supplied cannot be corroborated by other sources. Typically, newspaper reporters covering the incident, from the accident itself to its aftermath and on to the hearings, used the same sources for information, thus verifying them to the degree possible. That is not to say that such reports were always accurate, but when contradictions were found, a careful evaluation was made in determining what to select for inclusion in this book. The fact that Webb formally testified to the truth of his story lends it some credence, as does the presence at the hearing of the "charming and handsome" Miss Casey, the young woman he saved. But the action-packed account was not reprinted, as far as the author can tell, in any other publication then or in the years following. It is questionable enough *not* to be included in the narrative, yet quite possibly may be accurate. Perhaps it may still be verified.[3]

Cover of *Souvenir*, a yearbook about the activities of Company A, First Regiment, Minnesota National Guard in 1891

Webb, of Red Wing, reported he had advised several women aboard the *Sea Wing* to don life preservers as the storm clouds grew. Only one of them, Mary Casey—Webb calls her "May Casey," but the Memorial Booklet used "Mary"—followed his suggestion, putting on the "little reed appliance."

The witness continued, telling the inspectors, "I had scarcely fastened a preserver on when the first gale struck us. The next thing I realized I was floundering in the waves. A flash of lightening revealed the boat about fifty feet away and I swam toward her and seized Miss Casey. By this time the storm was upon us in all of its fury and I caught hold of the vessel's wheel [likely the steamer's paddle wheel] and… held on to the wheel with my right hand and kept hold of Miss Casey with my left. Pretty soon the boat partly righted and I was forced to let go."

The rolling action of the *Sea Wing* resulted in Mary Casey's life preserver ties being broken. Webb pressed on, "I believed she would be drowned, but did my best to keep her from sinking. We were about fifty feet from the boat and I could make little headway…Then I saw a kind of wooden floot [float] and we both seized it and were carried alongside the boat." They eventually reached safety.

Righting a Wrong

There is an enduring *Sea Wing* disaster-related legend that persisted in the Red Wing area for decades after the accident. A number of people with direct family connections to the calamity made the assertion that "city undertaker Allen" had a serious mental breakdown brought on by the stress of facing so many *Sea Wing* victims. Horace Anderson said Arland Allen "went a little berserk," Art Saupe wrote the "undertaker" became "mentally deranged," and Mathilda Staiger heard Allen "went crazy." Others interviewed for the book made similar assertions.[4]

The most credible source on this subject was Fred Kayser. His grandfather, Matthias Kayser, owned the Red Wing Furniture Company, which was known to provide casket construction and mortuary services. Matthias, along with his five sons—including Fred Kayser's father—"took over" funereal tasks when Allen, according to Fred, "had a breakdown." The Kaysers took this action at the request of Allen's wife, Anna. This Kayser account also notes that Allen had dealt with "the first group" of victims. Fatigue and overwhelming numbers certainly played a part in Allen's need for help. This book's narrative relies upon the Kayser family version of events.

Some existing records shed light on the subject. Goodhue County Coroner John Kyllo's handwritten "Reports" indicate to whom the bodies of the *Sea Wing* dead were delivered. Most, at first, were given to relatives, with "Father" typically the person receiving the victims. In such cases, the caretaker might have then sought mortuary help. Kyllo's notes show 19 of the dead sent to the town's two undertakers: 14 to the Kaysers and five to Allen. Many more would have arrived later without Kyllo's knowledge.

Clearly, the terrible events of July 13 placed a tremendous physical and psychological burden on Arland Allen. Still, Coroner Kyllo chose Allen's Main Street building as the site of an inquest on Tuesday evening, after a day filled with funerals. And Allen was appointed, along with six other civic leaders, to the General Decorating Committee for the memorial service on July 25.

It is possible that Allen temporarily buckled under the weight of responsibility, but it seems apparent he continued to perform his duties. He deserves credit for his work performed under extreme conditions.

Tracking the Rebuilt *Sea Wing*

John Norquist, the estimable historian of Diamond Bluff, Wisconsin—home to the *Sea Wing*—has reviewed the *Pierce County Herald* and other newspapers on both sides of the Mississippi looking for information about the community. One Norquist project was tracking David Wethern's rebuilt *Sea Wing* throughout the 1890s. He shared that helpful information with the author.[5] A sampling follows:

The Diamond Bluff headquarters of David Wethern's General Store and steamboat operation is today a bar and grill.

1893
April 27: Wethern pilots the *Sea Wing* to Red Wing's levee.

Dec. 7: An announcement is made that Wethern is buying new boilers for the *Sea Wing*.

1894
April 19: The refit of the *Sea Wing* will be completed by April 20.

April 23: The refitted *Sea Wing* makes a stop at Red Wing.

May 3: The *Sea Wing* stopped at Red Wing.

May 24: A news item notes that the *Sea Wing* will operate at La Crosse, Wisconsin.

Aug. 27: The *Sea Wing* is rafting on Lake Pepin.

1895
May 2: The *Sea Wing* has work in Stillwater, Minnesota.

1896
March 26: The *Sea Wing* is being repainted.

1899
April 6: Wethern will lease the *Sea Wing* to Capt. Hollingshead of Stillwater.

April 27: The *Sea Wing* arrives in St. Louis.

Nov. 16: Wethern is building a new steamboat called *Twin City*.

Wethern beached the *Sea Wing* in 1899 and used its engines and shafting for a larger steamboat he named *Twin City*. He used that sternwheeler for one season of rafting and then ran it as a packet, making scheduled runs between Wabasha and St. Paul. Just a year later he leased the vessel, and it was taken to southern Mississippi.

More From the Eliza Jane Crawford Letters

The letters written by H. W. Keller, the Hay Creek farmer and uncle to Holden schoolteacher and *Sea Wing* victim Eliza Jane Crawford, are among the few primary sources relating to the disaster that touch directly on the loss of a loved one. Keller's pain flows through his letter of July 15 (excerpted on page 79). Emotionally and physically exhausted from the long search and seemingly interminable wait, he anticipates word of his niece's fate and tries to comfort Eliza's parents.[6]

On July 27, Keller wrote another letter to Eliza's family that relates to the accident and provides detail about their daughter's time in Minnesota. A religious man, he notes that he and his wife declined their niece's invitation to join her on the *Sea Wing*. "I am superintending a Sunday school and I would not leave that if I even wanted to go," wrote Keller. He didn't blame Eliza for taking the excursion, "…for she was old enough to decide for herself," adding, "Don't blame her for going for there were many good people on the boat who lost their lives." Keller reported Katie Burkhard, Eliza's companion, "was of unquestionable character."

One of Keller's most difficult challenges was representing the family when Eliza's body was finally recovered. He related the grim details:

"She was not recognizable. Her dress that she was drowned in was left on for it could not be taken off also her shoes were left on. They might have been taken off. Her earrings were left in & I think one finger ring." After a detailed explanation of how he handled gathering his niece's belongings and settling her estate, he closed sadly:

"The hat she wore on the Excursion we found and will send. She bo't the hat here but the wreath she bro't from home. I cannot tell you how I feel when I see her things. I feel like saying many things but will not stir up your feelings more. I hope we may all meet her in a better life beyond this tear stained earth."

Eliza Jane Crawford wrote to her family about the joy she took from teaching her 32 eager young "Norwegian" students (Holden Township in Goodhue County was an enclave of Norwegian immigrants). In May 1890, after her first three months of teaching there, she penned about her students, "I think a great deal of them already and they appear to think the same of me." Crawford noted a charming classroom incident. She was reading by the fire before school when one of her young "scholars" came in and slowly crept near. "I raised my eyes from the book and then he slipped a handful of candy into my hand and ran out, before I could say anything to him."

The young schoolteacher also mentioned traveling to Red Wing for a teacher's meeting in early May. She had some photographs taken. It seems likely that one of them was used in the composite photo of *Sea Wing* victims.

Continuing Excursions

In 1935, respected Goodhue County and Red Wing historian Christian A. Rasmussen wrote of the *Sea Wing* disaster, "For more than ten years…it was impossible to interest the people of Red Wing and vicinity in any kind of river excursion."[7] Although there might have been reluctance among some, excursions did continue, along with the regularly scheduled runs of the Diamond Jo Line and Streckfus Company steamers.

Despite the horrific 1890 *Sea Wing* incident, the alluring riverboats and their promise of lazy summer days and romantic summer evenings cruising along the Mississippi continued to draw passengers. To many, the potential of accidents, though real, did not outweigh the appeal of river travel. Fear did not end the Steamboat Age. Train travel, along with the advent of the automobile, brought about its demise.

A group of excursionists stand on the Lake Pepin shoreline with a small steamer behind them.

Those Who Died

These 98 people died in the *Sea Wing* disaster. Their names and ages, if known, are those given in census, cemetery, church and death records.

A

Adams, Ella, 14, Mamie, 20, and Willie, 16, Trenton, WI
These children of Allen and Sarah Adams were cousins to John Adams and the Ways. Nine-year-old Myrtle stayed home.

Adams, John, 19, Hartland, WI
John, the son of James and Rebecca Adams, was a cousin to Ella, Mamie and Willie.

Anderson, Alexander O., 25, Belmont, ND
News accounts named Belmont as his hometown, while the coroner's report listed it as Buxton. He was aboard with fiancée, Randina Olson. Their wedding date was set for July 16. His body was the subject of the abortive coroner's inquest.

B

Bearson, Phoebe, 15, Red Wing, MN
Phoebe, the daughter of John and Betsy Bearson, is the only victim in the Kellogg composite whose photo was made postmortem.

Behrens, Dorothea, 33, and John, 33, Red Wing, MN
These immigrants from Germany are buried in St. John's Lutheran Cemetery.

Blaker, Phoebe, 35, Cena, 18, and Delbert, 15, Red Wing, MN
This is the family of William Blaker, who soon exonerated Captain Wethern in a statement to the newspapers.

Brenn, Louis, 25, Red Wing, MN
Louis, the son of George and Catherine Brenn, was among the last to be recovered. His body was found near Central Point on July 16.

Brown, Charles, 19, Red Wing, MN
Charles, the son of F. J. and Lucy Brown, was among the first of those recovered on July 14, after the *Sea Wing* had been partially righted.

Burkhard, Katie, 20, Hay Creek, MN
Katie, the daughter of Albert and Odelia Burkhard, is buried in Calvary Cemetery in Red Wing. She was the traveling companion of Eliza Crawford, a Holden teacher with relatives in Hay Creek.

C

Carlson, Joseph, 21, Red Wing, MN
Joseph was the son of prominent businessman and acting mayor G. A. Carlson. His body was the second to last found at Central Point. Viewing his badly disfigured remains was traumatic for his mother.

Christ, Fred J., 22, Red Wing, MN

This scion of a brewery-owning family in Red Wing's West End was one of three saloonkeepers who perished on the *Sea Wing*. The Christ family erected an impressive monument in Oakwood Cemetery.

Crawford, Eliza J., 27 (age supplied by family), Graysville, OH

Eliza taught school in Holden, MN, not far from Red Wing. Her letters, and those of her uncle in Hay Creek, are excerpted in this book.

D

Daily, Katie, 21, Red Wing, MN

Katie was the daughter of John and Kate Daily. No image of Katie was made available for the Kellogg composite photo.

Dinslage, Charles, 33, Red Wing, MN

Charles, the son of Henry and Francesca Dinslage, was a member of the Ancient Order of United Workmen. His was among the first of the many estates brought before Probate Judge Oscar Anderson.

F

Fisher, Minnie, 18, Red Wing, MN

Minnie was Mary Leach's friend. Mary missed the *Sea Wing* when it left Lake City. She was later shocked to see the body of her friend, Minnie, laid out with a large gash on the forehead.

Flynn, Mattie, 25, Trenton, WI

Mattie was on the *Sea Wing* with her fiancé Frank Way, who survived. She is buried in the Way family plot in Trenton.

Fulton, Ira, 37, Red Wing, MN

Fulton, an engineer at Red Wing Pottery, used his steam yacht to take friends to the Camp Lakeview program. He left the small steamer in Lake City for repair. He and his group boarded the *Sea Wing* for the return to Red Wing.

G

Gerken, Peter, 45, Maria, 39, Henry, 15, Emil, 13, Alvina, 10, Amandus, 7, and George, 5, Red Wing, MN

The family is buried under a single headstone in St. John's Lutheran Cemetery.

Green, Eliza (Mrs. Merritt), 36, and Ida, 18, Red Wing, MN

This mother and daughter were among the last to be recovered. Merritt Green claimed their bodies.

H

Harrison, Melissa, 17, Red Wing, MN

Melissa, the daughter of George and Lucretia Harrison, was incorrectly noted as "Meliza" in the coroner's report.

Hartman, George, 44, Red Wing, MN

Hartman, a successful German-born hardware dealer, settled in Hay Creek in 1856. He had moved to Red Wing, where he launched his hardware business.

Hattemer, Fred, 25, Florence Township, MN

Hattemer died on his 25th birthday. His body, along with that of his fiancée Annie Schneider, was found in the *Sea Wing's* cabin. They are buried in adjacent plots at St. John's Lutheran Cemetery.

Hempftling, Herman, 24, and Mary, 21, Red Wing, MN

Herman and Mary were newlyweds. Herman was a cousin to Frederick and Lizzie. There were two Mary Hempftlings killed—Mrs. Frederick Hempftling and Mrs. Herman Hempftling.

Hempftling, Mary, 43, Frederick, 19, and Lizzie, 17, Red Wing, MN

They were the family of Frederick Hempftling, Sr. George Diepenbrock reported he saw them near the *Sea Wing* galley just before the steamer capsized. Mary was Herman Hempftling's aunt (see entry above).

Holton, Mabel, 13, Red Wing, MN

Mabel's remains were found inside the cabin. The Lake City steamer *Ethel Howard* returned her body to Red Wing.

Horwedel, Theodor, 27, Red Wing, MN

Theodor is buried in Calvary Cemetery. At the time of this accident, his fiancée was traveling from Germany by ship to join him.

Humpert, Johanna, 23, Red Wing, MN

Johanna was the widowed daughter of Christ and Sophia Schulenberg. She was buried in the same St. John's Cemetery grave as her mother and two younger siblings. [This is a correction of the 1986 book entry for Humpert.]

I

Ingebretson, Edward, 18, Red Wing, MN

The son of Christopher and Serena Ingebretson, Edward was listed in some reports as "Hamberson" or "Christopherson."

Ingebretson, John, 13, Red Wing, MN

John, son of Ole and Helga Ingebretson, was a paperboy for the *Daily Republican*. No photo of him appears in the Kellogg composite view.

J

Johnson, Corden, 25, Trenton, WI

Johnson's body was among those recovered at Central Point on the first day. He is buried in Trenton Cemetery.

Jurgensen, Willie, Diamond Bluff, WI

Willie, son of Danish-immigrant shoemaker Hans Jurgensen, a survivor of the accident, is not shown in the Kellogg composite photograph.

K

Kremer, Leon, and Millie, 40, Diamond Bluff, WI

Their bodies were found separately, with Millie's discovered near Central Point on July 16. The Goodhue County coroner in Red Wing issued their death certificates.

L

Larson, Mrs. Ed, 35, Red Wing, MN

Larson's was one of the first bodies recovered. Her husband claimed her remains but, since he was unable to pay for burial, Goodhue County covered the charges.

Leeson, Thomas, 17, Red Wing, MN

Thomas, the son of Robert and Alice Leeson, was among the first recovered.

Lillyblad, Lenus, 10, Red Wing, MN

Lenus was the son of well-known grocery and clothing storekeeper Gust Lillyblad. He loaded ice onto the *Sea Wing* and accepted free passage.

M

Mero, Roderic L., 51, Austin, 19, and Myrtle, 14, Diamond Bluff, WI

The members of this farm family were related by marriage to Captain Wethern. The father and son were seen clinging to wreckage. Their bodies, recovered on Wednesday, July 16, had been battered by hail. Myrtle had been found Monday morning.

N

Nelson, Emma C., Red Wing, MN

Emma worked at Berquist Drug Store. Apparently, she was among those who died in the *Sea Wing's* cabin. Her body was among the first returned to Red Wing on Monday morning.

Nelson, George, 29, Red Wing, MN

George, the son of Frank and Caroline Nelson, was a barber. His body was taken to "undertaker Allyn" (Arland H. Allen).

Nelson, Mary, 37, Red Wing, MN

Mary was the wife of Ole Nelson. They lived at 613 Plum Street.

Newton, Henry, 14, Red Wing, MN

Henry was the son of George and Sarah Newton. He was eventually found near Central Point on July 16.

Niles, Millie, 16, Diamond Bluff, WI

Millie was the sister of the Niles crew members, a cousin to Captain Wethern, and was related to Mel Sparks through marriage. All of her relatives aboard the ship survived.

O

Olson, Mary, 16, Red Wing, MN

Mary's body was in the first group of bodies returned to Red Wing.

Olson, Peter, 30, Red Wing, MN

Peter's remains were positively identified because of the inscription on the gold ring he wore. The *St. Paul Dispatch* of July 17, 1890, reported his finger was amputated to get the ring off, while the *Pioneer Press* said the ring was cut off.

Olson, Randina, 24, Red Wing, MN

Randina was onboard with her fiancé, Alexander O. Anderson. Her body was found on July 16, the day they had planned to marry.

O'Shaughnessy, Martin, 26, Welch, MN
    Martin was honored in a poem by an anonymous friend who wrote that
    Martin's only fear was of water.
Oskey, Oren, 17, Red Wing, MN
    Oren jumped off the barge *Jim Grant* with his friend Charles Lidberg, who
    survived. Oskey was wearing a life preserver.

P

Palmer, Alice, 20, and Nettie, 18, Trenton, WI
    The women's bodies were found inside the *Sea Wing*. Guardsmen recovered
    Alice's remains after chopping holes in the cabin roof. Nettie's body was found
    after the steamer was righted on July 14.
Persig, Julia, 29, and Anna, 26, Hay Creek, MN
    The sisters were aboard the steamboat with men friends. Julia was identified by
    articles on her body and was among the last recovered.
Peterson, Charles, 16, Red Wing, MN
    The son of Charles and Wilda Peterson was found in the early morning hours
    of July 16 when his body surfaced off Central Point.
Peterson, Knute, 30, Red Wing, MN
    Knute's body was found on July 14 and was one of those wearing a life preserver.
    His watch had stopped at 11:50. He was to marry a Miss Johnson, who was so
    "crazed with grief" at his death that "permanent insanity" was feared.

R

Rehder, Rosa, 11, and Johann "Henry," 8, Red Wing, MN
    These were the children of Claus Henry and Anna Rehder. Henry was found the
    first day. Rosa was the last of the 98 victims recovered. Their father led the *Sea
    Wing* four-piece orchestra, so these two siblings traveled with their uncle, aunt,
    and cousins, the Gerkens.

S

Scherf, Martin, 23, Hay Creek, MN
    Martin was the son of Anton Scherf, who recovered, repaired and wore
    Martin's watch for years. He was buried in an expensive ($45) coffin.
Scherf, Mary, 36, and Hattie, 16, Red Wing, MN
    Mary and Hattie were the wife and daughter of saloon owner Fred Scherf, who
    survived.
Schneider, Annie, 19, Red Wing, MN
    Annie, the daughter of Adam and Rosa Schneider, was buried at St. John's
    Lutheran Cemetery adjacent to her fiancé, Fred Hattemer.
Schoeffler, John, Kate, 25, John, Jr., 6, and Frederick, 6 months, Red Wing, MN
    The ages listed here are from the coroner's report. This was John Schoeffler's
    second family. Kate was found holding her infant son. William, John's son
    from his first marriage, was at home.

Schulenberg, Sophia, 40, Henry, 11, and Minna, 7, Red Wing, MN
This was the family of Christ Schulenberg. Sophia was found in the first hours after the accident; Henry and Minna on July 16. The Schulenberg's widowed daughter, Johanna Humpert, also drowned. None of the members of this family are pictured in the Kellogg composite photo of victims.

Seavers, Fred, 50, and Ida, 16, Red Wing, MN
Ida was the third victim recovered from the cabin on July 14. Her father, Fred, had been a blacksmith. Her brother George, 17, paired with Boze Adams, and the two floated together in life preservers and reached safety.

Skoglund, Mary, 17, Red Wing, MN
Not found until July 16, Mary's body was transferred to Stockholm, WI, for burial at the request of Lake City attorney Wesley Kinney.

Smith, Florence, 28, Diamond Bluff, WI
Florence is buried in the Diamond Bluff Cemetery not far from the Sparks and Wethern family graves.

Staiger, Annie, 20, and Frances, 18, Florence Township, MN
Annie and Frances, the daughters of John and Victoria Staiger, were on board the *Sea Wing* with Frank Lampman and Ed Stevens. The young men tried, but failed, to save them. Their wake was held at the Haustein residence in Red Wing.

Steffenson, Henry, 18, Red Wing, MN
Henry was the son of Ole Steffenson.

Strope, John F., 14, Red Wing, MN
John was also listed in news reports as "Stroup" and by the coroner as "Straub." His father was called Stroupe. *Those Who Perished* spelled his name "Strope."

V

Vieths, Friedrika, "Rikka," 10, Red Wing, MN
Her remains were identified by her father, Kasper, at the Red Wing levee. She is listed in St. John's Lutheran Church records as "Friedrika."

W

Way, Adda, 21, and Ednah, 14, Trenton, WI
Adda and Ednah were the daughters of Benjamin Way, who closed the Trenton post office and sold his store after their deaths. They were cousins to the Adams victims. Their brother, Frank, survived.

Wethern, Nellie Boyes, 31, and Perley, 8, Diamond Bluff, WI
Capt. David Wethern's wife and son perished. His son, Roy, survived.

Wilson, James, 40, Trenton, WI
James's body was among the last recovered at Central Point.

Winter, Bertha, 13, Red Wing, MN
Bertha's body was found near a hole chopped in the cabin roof and was taken ashore with her face covered by a piece of the *Sea Wing's* flag.

Those Who Survived

This list of *Sea Wing* accident survivors uses the names compiled in the memorial booklet *In Memory of Those Who Perished*. It includes only those onboard for the return trip from Lake City to Red Wing.

A

Adams, Robert, Lake City, MN
Ake, Axel, Red Wing, MN
Ammon, John, Red Wing, MN
Anderberg, John, Red Wing, MN
Anderson, Arthur, Red Wing, MN
Appenzeller, Jacob, Red Wing, MN
Axelson, Ernest, Red Wing, MN

B

Bartron, Aggie, Red Wing, MN
Bartron, Guy, Red Wing, MN
Bayrell, L. D., Red Wing, MN
Bayrell, Leo S., Argyle, MN
Beckmark, Gust, Red Wing, MN
Berlin, Oscar, Red Wing, MN
Blaker, William, Red Wing, MN
Boner, Emma, Burnside, MN
Boner, John, Burnside, MN
Boner, W., Burnside, MN
Bowman, Oscar, Red Wing, MN
Burke, E. P., Diamond Bluff, WI

C

Callisehan, Thomas, Burnside, MN
Carlstrom, Albert, Red Wing, MN
Carroll, Charles, Red Wing, MN
Carver, Will, Lake City, MN
Casey, Mary, Red Wing, MN
Chellstrom, Frederick, Red Wing, MN
Chellstrom, Robert, Red Wing, MN
Cook, George H., Red Wing, MN

D

Danielson, E. T., Red Wing, MN
Dannum, Richard, Red Wing, MN

DeKay, Will W., Red Wing, MN
Diepenbrock, George, Jr.,
  Red Wing, MN

E

Eisenbrand, George, Red Wing, MN
Eisenbrand, Robert, Red Wing, MN
Eisenbrand, W. J., Red Wing, MN

F

Fisher, Charles, Red Wing, MN
Forsell, Oscar, Red Wing, MN
Freeman, Vic, Red Wing, MN

G

Gartland, Francis P.,
  Diamond Bluff, WI
Gilbertson, John, Red Wing, MN

H

Hawkins, George, Red Wing, MN
Hawkins, George, Jr., Red Wing, MN
Heckstrom, Peter, Prairie Island, MN
Heidenreich, Charles, Red Wing, MN
Herder, Hugo, Red Wing, MN
Hill, Edward, Diamond Bluff, WI
Hill, Flora (Mrs. Hiram), Diamond
  Bluff, WI
Hill, Maria, Diamond Bluff, WI
Hope, Charles, Diamond Bluff, WI
Hope, Frank, Diamond Bluff, WI
Hope, Henry, Diamond Bluff, WI

J

Jacoby, C. D., Red Wing, MN
Johnson, Albert, Red Wing, MN

Johnson, C. A., Red Wing, MN
Johnson, R. F., Red Wing, MN
Johnson, Theodore, Red Wing, MN

K

Kempe, Theodore F., Red Wing, MN
Kenney, Will, Red Wing, MN
Kolberg, Alfred, Red Wing, MN
Kronberg, Alfred, Red Wing, MN
Kronberg, Charles, Red Wing, MN

L

Lampman, Frank C., Minneapolis, MN
Landeck, George, Red Wing, MN
Lees, A. F., Red Wing, MN
Lidberg, Charles A., Red Wing, MN
Luft, Henry, Red Wing, MN

M

Mabey, Henry, Lake City, MN
Malm, Peter, Red Wing, MN
Martinson, Ed E., Red Wing, MN
Mehrkens, Eddie, Red Wing, MN
Mero, Frank, Minneapolis, MN
Minder, Theodore, Lake City, MN
Monson, Andrew, Red Wing, MN
Morris, E. D., Red Wing, MN
Mueller, Charles, Red Wing, MN

N

Neil, Charles, Diamond Bluff, WI
Nelson, Axel, Red Wing, MN
Nelson, Hendrick, Red Wing, MN
Niles, Edmund, Diamond Bluff, WI
Niles, Harry, Diamond Bluff, WI
Niles, William, Diamond Bluff, WI

O

Olson, August, Red Wing, MN
Oss, Jens, Red Wing, MN

P

Palmer, Frances, Trenton, WI
Palmer, Perley, Trenton, WI

Patterson, William, Red Wing, MN
Perkins, Frank, Red Wing, MN
Plaas, William, Red Wing, MN
Purdy, Samuel H., Red Wing, MN
Purdy, William, Red Wing, MN

Q

Qual, John, Red Wing, MN

R

Reeve, George, Red Wing, MN
Rehder, Henry, Red Wing, MN
Rock, Ludwig, Red Wing, MN

S

Sandstrom, Claus, Red Wing, MN
Schenach, Ed, Red Wing, MN
Scherf, Fred, Red Wing, MN
Scriber, Andrew, Trenton, WI
Seastrand, Herman, Red Wing, MN
Seavers, George, Red Wing, MN
Simmons, N. K., Red Wing, MN
Simon, Otto, Red Wing, MN
Smith, George, Red Wing, MN
Sparks, (Mrs.) Ellie, Diamond Bluff, WI
Sparks, Jesse, Diamond Bluff, WI
Sparks, Marion L., Diamond Bluff, WI
Sparks, Warren, Diamond Bluff, WI
Sparks, William, Diamond Bluff, WI
Stevens, Ed, Minneapolis, MN
Sultzer, C. S., Red Wing, MN

T

Thompson, George, Red Wing, MN
Truttman, Charles, Red Wing, MN

W

Ward, Sherman, Red Wing, MN
Way, Frank, Trenton, WI
Webb, James, Red Wing, MN
Wethern, Capt. David Niles,
    Diamond Bluff, WI
Wethern, Roy, Diamond Bluff, WI

Acknowledgments

There is a growing legion of local historians in Minnesota and Wisconsin and, over the years, I have had the good fortune to work with a number of them. A few receive small stipends for their efforts, but most work as volunteers in the service of history. They nurture and refresh a collective community memory by preserving records of the past, creating new areas of study and developing interpretive analysis of existing material. It is to a cadre of such overlooked friends of history who assisted in this expanded edition of the *Sea Wing Disaster* that I owe a first debt of gratitude.

In Lake City, Don Schwartz, the volunteer curator of the Lake City Historical Society archives, assisted me in searching that important resource. Schwartz not only helped in gathering the society's materials over the years, he carefully organized them into an accessible depository. He granted use of a number of outstanding turn-of-the-twentieth-century photographs featuring Lake City and Lake Pepin that enhanced the visual record and the book.

Ben Threinen, veteran Twin Cities television videographer and Lake City resident, along with Bob Norberg, vice president of the Lake City Historical Society, forged a valuable and useful *Sea Wing* alliance with me. The Lake Citians sought my help for a video that they were preparing about the *Sea Wing* disaster. Soon, we were assisting each other, sharing research and ideas. Ours has been a most enjoyable and mutually beneficial relationship.

In Wisconsin, Pat Mory of the Pierce County Historical Association, a modest-sized but ambitious Ellsworth-based organization, offered use of their archives. She proved particularly useful in gathering family data as well as photos of Diamond Bluff and Trenton residents involved in the *Sea Wing* disaster. Mory's enthusiasm for the project, combined with her knowledge of local resources, produced excellent results.

John Norquist is also active in the Pierce County history group, but, singlehandedly, he *is* the Diamond Bluff Historical Society. A resident of that small Mississippi River community, John has studied its history in minute detail. His personal walking tour of the city and excellent background information on Captain David Wethern and his family—the Meros, Sparks and Niles as well—was most profitable.

Dr. Thomas A. Hodgson grew up on Lake Pepin and, starting as a child, boated on the lake throughout his life. His broad interest in boating—he worked in yacht race management for 40 years as a professional and volunteer—led him to a study of the *Sea Wing* and its fate. A portion of his insightful 1990 investigation, "A Meteorological Look at the Sea Wing Disaster," is featured, with his permission, in the Epilogue. Hodgson's analysis brings weather conditions at the time of the accident into sharper focus. Also included in this book is the map he developed to plot the steamboat's course on the evening of July 13, 1890. This Lake Pepin view includes a well-reasoned estimate regarding the location of the tragic accident. Tom

Hodgson's outstanding research adds clarity to important aspects of the *Sea Wing* disaster. He has my gratitude for sharing this valuable analysis.

The Goodhue County Historical Society (GCHS), founded in 1869 and Minnesota's *first* such history group, is a much larger organization than those mentioned previously, but it provides the same kind of personal service to those researching its collections. GCHS's history center is the major repository of *Sea Wing* related documents, photographs, letters and realia. Librarian Diane Buganski and Collections/Exhibits Manager Johanna Grothe make the Society's collections easily accessible and can be counted upon for productive suggestions.

The Minnesota Historical Society's History Center (MHS) in St. Paul, and its many specialists, allow easy entrée to its invaluable collections. The staff and the facility itself make conducting research at MHS a pleasure. Likewise, staff members of the University of Minnesota's Wilson Library were most accommodating in facilitating our research.

Red Wing's Captain Rusty Mathiasmeier has made it a mission to keep the *Sea Wing* story alive through his boat tours of the Mississippi River and Lake Pepin. I was fortunate to be among those benefitting from his informative *Sight-Sea-Er II* voyages.

We appreciate the efforts of those who provided images that promote a better understanding of the *Sea Wing* story. Caleb Johnson shared his genealogical studies and photographs of Diamond Bluff's Mero family. Larry Nielson, who operates Lake City's *Pearl of the Lake*, provided access to his remarkable collection of Lake Pepin photos. Steve Kohn, assistant planner for the city of Red Wing, helped procure present-day images of that community.

Several individuals deserve special mention for their valued assistance with this project. In 2008, Char Henn, then director of the Goodhue County Historical Society, began efforts to get an expanded version of the 1986 *The Sea Wing Disaster* into print. Char also became the indexer for this book. Amy Nelson was GCHS acting director when a renewed effort for a reprint began in 2013; she was encouraging and quickly "on board." Charles O. Richardson, a longtime supporter of Red Wing and Goodhue County history, provided constructive advice to move the project forward.

Since this book is an expanded version of the 1986 book *The Sea Wing Disaster*, it is appropriate that those people who helped with getting the first edition into print again be recognized.

Here, in full, is that original Acknowledgment:

To the many people who helped me with this project, my sincere thanks, especially Fred "Scoop" Jonson, a retired Red Wing newspaper reporter who read the manuscript and personally solicited support for the project. Thomas C. Thompson, a Minnesota Historical Society staff member living in Red Wing, provided prepublication expertise and spent many hours shepherding this book through its final phases. Ellen B. Green, the book's editor and publication manager, took a personal interest in the manuscript and always displayed professionalism and good judgment.

I am grateful to the Goodhue County Historical Society (GCHS) for its faith in publishing this history as its first attempt at such a project. Orville Olson and Jean Chesley were unflagging supporters during the three-year journey to publication. Their enthusiasm was equaled by other staff members who freely gave both time and expertise. GCHS president Richard Johnson finalized arrangements with Loren Hamre on behalf of Roy and Merle Meyer, who provided the necessary financial support for this publication.

Many people responded to my early requests for information with personal stories, greatly adding to the human appeal of the book. Horace Anderson, Roy Anderson, Frances Baker, Jay Carlson, Robert Carlson, Chuck Francis, Elayne Galvin, Blanche and Arnold Harding, Fred Kayser, Edna Martenson, Myrtle Martenson, Mathilda Staiger Metzler, Art Saupe, and Dorothy Winjum granted interviews. E. H. Burke, Emma Lark, Marcella Johnson, and Mary Lee Stevens wrote to me with their stories.

Librarians, archivists, staff researchers, audio-visual experts, cartographers, and other staff members from organizations on both sides of the Mississippi River provided valuable research assistance, particularly those at the Minnesota Historical Society, University of Minnesota Libraries, Red Wing Public Library, St. Croix Valley Research Center at the University of Wisconsin-River Falls, Wabasha County Historical Society, and Washington County Historical Society. Red Wing city officials such as the late mayor Ed Powderly (also my high school history and journalism teacher) and city clerk Burton Will were helpful, making available early records and council proceedings and saving much time.

I valued the help of my father, Fred Johnson, Sr., who carefully read the narrative, offering ideas for clarification and improvement, and the support of my mother, Mary Johnson, who has liked everything I've written since kindergarten. My wife, Diane Johnson, helped with interviews and record searches as research assistant, corrected mistakes and improved my writing style as in-home editor, and hammered out successive drafts as secretary-typist. She put up with the incredible clutter of my office, the only blot on an otherwise perfectly organized household, and she kept the project alive, encouraging me when publishing prospects were bleak and I became discouraged. Without her support, this book might never have been completed.

Image Credits

Author's Collection—39, 54 bottom, 55, 59, 62, 68, 69 top and bottom, 71, 72, 75, 85, 87 top, 88, 91, 97, 103, 107, 109 top, 112, 117, 118, 119 top, 121, 123, 125

Ben Thrienen Collection—56

Caleb H. Johnson Private Collection—26, 77

City of Red Wing—69 middle, 119 bottom

David Thofern Collection—30–31, 40, 119 top

Edna Martenson Collection—78

Goodhue County Historical Society—8, 20–21, 22, 27, 28, 29 top, 34 top, 35, 41, 42 top, 43 top, 44, 45, 46, 47 top, 48 top, 49, 53, 54 top, 57 top, 63, 66, 67, 74, 76, 79, 80, 81, 82, 92, 93, 95, 96, 100, 101, 105, 108, 109 bottom, 114, 115 middle, 116, 120

Lake City Historical Society— 6, 36–37, 50, 52, 83, 84, 127

Minnesota Historical Society—13 Fred A. Bill Collection, 15, 16, 17, 24, 29 bottom, 32, 34 bottom, 57 bottom, 115 bottom

Pierce County Historical Association—23, 25, 43 bottom

University of Minnesota Wilson Library—60, 61, 64–65, 73

US Geological Survey (Maps)—18–19, 33

Winona County Historical Society—14

Bibliography

Books, Articles, Pamphlets

"A Visit to Frontenac and Lake Pepin." *American Traveller's Journal* 2 (August 1881).

Allen, Ken. *Old Frontenac Minnesota: Its History and Architecture*. Charleston, SC: History Press, 2011.

Along the Mississippi on the Diamond Jo Line Steamers. St. Louis: Diamond Jo Line Steamers, 1908.

Ames, Frederick W. *Historical Sketch and Souvenir, Company A 1ˢᵗ Infantry, NGSM*. Minneapolis: Swinburne Printing, 1891.

Andreas, A. T. *An Illustrated Atlas of the State of Minnesota*. Chicago: A. T. Andreas, 1874.

Anfinson, John O. *The River of History: A Historic Resources Study of the Mississippi National River and Recreation Area*. St. Paul: US Army Corps of Engineers, St. Paul District, 2003.

— "The Secret History of the Mississippi's Earliest Locks and Dams." *Minnesota History* 54 Summer 1995.

Angell, Madeline. *Red Wing, Minnesota: Saga of a River Town*. Minneapolis: Dillon Press, 1977.

Berman, Bruce. *Encyclopedia of American Shipwrecks*. Boston: Mariners Press, 1972.

Blair, Walter A. *A Raft Pilot's Log: A History of the Great Rafting Industry on the Upper Mississippi, 1840–1915*. Cleveland: Arthur H. Clark Co., 1930.

Blegen, Theodore C. *Minnesota: A History of the State*. Minneapolis: University of Minnesota Press, 1963.

Bowen, Dana T. *Shipwrecks of the Lakes*. Daytona Beach: Published by the author, 1952.

Brisbin, James S. *Souvenir of Red Wing, Minnesota*. Red Wing: Red Wing Printing Co., 1891.

Clark, W. D. *Rest Island and Lake City Souvenir*. Lake City: June 1892.

Curtiss-Wedge, Franklyn. *History of Dakota and Goodhue Counties, Minnesota*. Chicago: H. C. Cooper, Jr., & Co., 1910.

—. *History of Goodhue County, Minnesota*. Chicago: H. C. Cooper, Jr., & Co., 1909.

—. *History of Wabasha County*. Winona, MN: H. C. Cooper, Jr., & Co., 1920.

Easton, Augustus B. *History of the St. Croix Valley*, Vol. 1. Chicago: H. C. Cooper, Jr., & Co., 1909.

Ericson, Kathryn, ed., *Map of Goodhue County Minnesota, 1877*. Red Wing: Goodhue County Historical Society, 1991. Reprint of Warner & Foote's 1877 county map.

Forslund, Mrs. Eric W. and E. D. J. Larson. *Stockholm's Saga: Being the History of the Village of Stockholm-on-Lake Pepin, Pepin County, Wisconsin and Vicinity*. Pepin: Pepin *Herald*, 1941.

Friends of Lake City Library, *Lake City Remembers*. Lake City: 2006.

Haines, C. J. and E. G. Dean. *A Souvenir of Lake City, Minnesota Including Frontenac, Villa Maria and Rest Island*. Lake City: H. A. Young & Co. and Jewell Nursery, 1897.

Hancock, J. W. *History of Goodhue County, Minnesota, by an Old Settler*. Red Wing: Red Wing Printing Co., 1893.

Hankins, Ross. "Excursion Boats on the Upper Mississippi, 1910–1927," manuscript, Goodhue County Historical Society collections.

Harris, Dolores Haustein. "Writer's grandfather gives firsthand account of historic tragedy." *Generations of Today*, July 2000.

Hartsough, Mildred L. *From Canoe to Steel Barge on the Upper Mississippi*. Minneapolis: University of Minnesota Press, 1934.

Historical Sketch of the First Regiment & Infantry, National Guard, State of Minnesota. Washington DC: Librarian of Congress, 1882.

History of Northern Wisconsin. Chicago: Western Historical Co., 1881.

Hunter, Louis C. with Beatrice Jones Hunter. *Steamboats on the Western Rivers: An Economic and Technological History*. Cambridge: Harvard University Press, 1949.

Imholte, John Quinn. *The First Volunteers*. Minneapolis: Ross E. Haines, 1963.

Johnson, Frederick, L. *Goodhue County, Minnesota: A Narrative History*. Red Wing: Goodhue County Historical Society, 2000.

—. "Unlocking the Mysteries of the Sea Wing." *Minnesota History* 52 Summer 1990.

—. "When the Trail Runs Cold: Researching the Story of The *Sea Wing* Disaster." *Minnesota Genealogist* 27 September 1996. [Transcription of a June 15, 1996, speech presented to the Minnesota Genealogical Society].

Lloyd, James T. *Lloyd's Steamboat Directory and Disasters on the Western Waters*. Cincinnati: James T. Lloyd & Co., 1856.

Loehr, Rodney C. "Caleb Door and the Early Minnesota Lumber Industry." *Minnesota History* 24 June 1943.

Mahoney, Timothy R. *River Towns in the Great West: The Structure of Provincial Urbanization in the American Midwest, 1820–1870*, 166. Cambridge, UK: Cambridge University Press, 2002.

Marshall, Albert M. *Goodhue County's First Hundred Years*. Red Wing: *Daily Republican Eagle*, 1954.

Meister, Mark J. "The Man Who Painted the Lake Gervais Tornado." *Minnesota History* 45 Winter 1977.

Meyer, Roy W. *The Ghost Towns & Discontinued Post Offices of Goodhue County*. Red Wing: Goodhue County Historical Society, 2003.

Nash and Morgan. *Atlas of Pierce County, Wisconsin*. Appleton: 1877–8.

Paskoff, Paul F. *Troubled Waters: Steamboat Disasters, River Improvements and American Public Policy, 1821–1861*. Baton Rouge: LSU Press, 2007.

"Pearl of Pepin: A Beautiful Lake City is Progressing Along Modern Lines." *Western Magazine* 8 November 1916.

Peterson, Ursula, editor. "The *Sea Wing* Disaster," *Pierce County Heritage* 2 Summer 1996.

Peterson, William J. "Captains and Cargoes of Early Upper Mississippi Steamboats." *Wisconsin Magazine of History* 13 1929–1930.

Potter, Merle. *101 Best Stories of Minnesota*. Minneapolis: Harrison & Smith, 1931.

Quick, Herbert and Edward. *Mississippi Steamboatin'*. New York: Holt and Co., 1926.

Rasmussen, Christian A. *History of Goodhue County, Minnesota*. Red Wing: Published by the author, 1935.

—. *History of Red Wing, Minnesota*. Red Wing: Published by the author, 1934.

Red Wing Printing Co.'s Complete Directory of Red Wing, 1894. Red Wing: Red Wing Printing Co.

Rosenberger, Jesse L. *Through Three Centuries*. Chicago: University of Chicago Press, 1922.

St. John's Lutheran Church. Official Records of Ministrations of the St. John's Lutheran Church, Book II. Red Wing.

Short, Lloyd M. *Steamboat Inspection Service*. New York: Appleton & Co., 1922.

Smith, Frederick L. *The History of Frontenac*. Frontenac, MN: Privately published, 1951.

Toensing, W. F. *Minnesota Congressmen, Legislators, and Other Elected Officials*. St. Paul: Minnesota Historical Society, 1971.

Watson, Bruce F. *Weather Guide*. Navarre, MN: Freshwater Biological Research Foundation, 1976.

Way, Frederick, Jr. *Way's Packet Directory, 1848–1983*. Athens: Ohio University, 1983.

Woodward, I. B. ed. *Historical Sketch and Souvenir First Battalion Artillery NGSM, Battery A*. Minneapolis: Miller Printing, 1892.

Woolley, John G. editor, *The Rest Islander* 1 Rest Island, MN: October 1893.

Government Records and Documents

Biennial Report of the Adjutant General of Minnesota for the Two Years Ending July 31,1890. Minneapolis: Harrison and Smith, Printers, 1891.

Department of Commerce and Labor, Steamboat Inspection Service. *General Rules and Regulations Prescribed by the Board of Supervising Inspectors*. Washington DC: Government Printing Office, 1910.

Department of Commerce and Steamboat Inspection Service. *General Rules and Regulations Prescribed by the Board of Supervising Inspectors, Lakes Other than Great Lakes, Bays and Sounds*. Washington DC: Government Printing Office, 1916.

Goodhue County. Register of Deaths. Goodhue County Courthouse, Red Wing.

Haugen, Nils P. Papers. St. Croix Valley Research Center, University of Wisconsin-River Falls.

In Memory of Those Who Perished in the Disaster to the Steamer Sea Wing on Lake Pepin, July, 13, 1890. Red Wing: Red Wing Printing Co., 1890.

Metcalf, V. T. *General Rules and Regulations Prescribed by the Board of Supervising Inspectors as Amended January 1906.* Washington DC: Government Printing Office, 1906.

Minnesota Adjutant General's Office. "A History of the Minnesota National Guard," manuscript, St. Paul: State of Minnesota, 1940.

Red Wing. *Record of Proceedings of the City Council of the City of Red Wing Minnesota, Book E, 1888–1892.* Red Wing: Red Wing Printing Co.

St. Paul District, Corps of Engineers. *Old Man River: 50th Anniversary, Nine-Foot Navigation Channel, Upper Mississippi River, 1938–1988.* St. Paul: Corps of Engineers, May 1998.

State of Wisconsin. *Public Documents of the State of Wisconsin*, vol 2. Madison: 1903. "Table IV: Population of Wisconsin, 1890, 1900, 1895."

Supervising Inspector-General of Steam Vessels. *Laws Governing the Steamboat Inspection Service*, as amended January, 1882-'83-'84-'87. Washington: Government Printing Office, 1887.

US Census Office. *Tenth Census of the United States, 1880.* (Goodhue County, MN and Pierce County, WI) Washington DC

—. *Twelfth Census of the United States, 1900.* (Goodhue County, MN. and Pierce County, WI) Washington DC

US Treasury Department, Steamboat Inspection Service. *Report of the Board of Supervising Inspectors of Steam Vessels* (National Archives T 38.10:1891). Washington D.C: 1891.

Willard, S. J. Annual Report of the City Clerk: *Financial Statement*, year ending April 30, 1891.

Minnesota Historical Society

Bill, Fred A. ed., Draft of Stephen B. Hanks, *Memoirs of Captain Stephen B. Hanks.* Fred A. Bill and Family Papers, Minnesota Historical Society, St. Paul.

District Court (Goodhue County). Coroner's Records, 1867–1975. "Coroner's Inquest Registers, 1890."

—. "Coroner's Reports, 1890."

Roy H. Wethern Papers, Minnesota Historical Society, St. Paul, MN.

Newspapers

All Minnesota newspapers listed can be found in microform at the Minnesota Historical Society in St. Paul. The *Pierce County Herald* is also available in microform at the St. Croix Valley Research Center, University of Wisconsin-River Falls.

Lake City *Graphic Sentinel.* Weekly, April–September 1890.

Minneapolis Journal. Daily, July–September 1890.

Minneapolis Tribune. Daily, July–September 1890.

Pierce County Herald (Ellsworth, WI). Weekly, July–August 1890.

Red Wing *Advance Sun.* Weekly, April–September 1890.

Red Wing *Argus.* Weekly, April–September 1890.

Red Wing *Daily Republican.* March–October 1890.

Red Wing Daily Republican Eagle. 1957, 1958, 1960, 1971, 1973.

Red Wing *Journal.* Weekly, April–October 1890.

St. Paul *Daily Globe.* July–September 1890.

St. Paul Dispatch. Daily, July–September 1890.

St. Paul *Pioneer Press.* Daily, July–September 1890.

Winona *Daily Republican.* July–August 1890.

Endnotes

Abbreviations in notes are:

GCHS for Goodhue County Historical Society
LCGS for Lake City *Graphic Sentinel*
PCH for *Pierce County Herald*
RWA for Red Wing *Argus*
RWAS for Red Wing *Advance Sun*

RWDR for Red Wing *Daily Republican*
RWDRE for Red Wing *Daily Republican Eagle*
SPD for *St. Paul Dispatch*
SPDG for St. Paul *Daily Globe*
SPPP for St. Paul *Pioneer Press*

Prologue

1. "Terrible Catastrophe, Steamer Galena Burned to the Water's Edge, Five Lives lost, Mails, Freight and Baggage Totally Destroyed," *Red Wing Republican*, July 1, 1858, 1. "Burning of the Steamer Galena, Thrilling Account by a Passenger," *New York Times*, July 17, 1858, carried this *Chicago Press and Tribune* account. It is also found in Franklyn W. Curtiss-Wedge, *History of Goodhue County, Minnesota* (Chicago: H. C. Cooper, Jr. & Son, 1909) 491–492. Robert C. Toole, "Competition and Consolidation: The Galena Packet Co., 1847–63," *Journal of the Illinois State Historical Society* 57 (Autumn 1964): 229–234.

2. "Terrible Catastrophe," July 1, 1858, 1. Captain Russell Blakeley, "The Commerce of Civilization," *Collections of the Minnesota Historical Society* (8, 1898): 405–406. Timothy R. Mahoney, *River Towns in the Great West: The Structure of Provincial Urbanization in the American Midwest, 1820–1870*, 166. (Cambridge, UK: Cambridge University Press, 2002) 126. *Goodhue County Republican*, March 23, 1860, 3. "Burning of the Steamer Galena, *New York Times*, July 17, 1858.

3. Draft of Stephen B. Hanks, *Memoirs of Captain Stephen B. Hanks*, edited by Fred A. Bill, c. 1925, 165–166, Fred A. Bill and Family Papers, Minnesota Historical Society, St. Paul. The extensive Hanks diaries, dictated during the years 1904–1908, are also found in the Bill papers. Bill edited the diaries into a 1926 *Saturday Evening Post* series "The Life and Adventures of Capt. Stephen B. Hanks, A Cousin of Abraham Lincoln, and a Pilot and Captain on the Upper Mississippi River for Seventy-Two Years." See "News and Comment," *Minnesota History Bulletin* 4 (February–May, 1921–1922): 88 for information about Bill and the Hanks memoirs. Two years passed before local civic leaders and the *Galena's* owner, Galena, Dubuque, Dunleith and Minnesota Packet Line, combined to remove the sunken wreckage from the Red Wing levee.

4. "Hanks, *Memoirs*, 166. Curtiss-Wedge, *History of Goodhue County*, 494. The five victims of the accident were buried at Red Wing's Oakwood Cemetery.

5. Louis C. Hunter with Beatrice Jones Hunter, *Steamboats on the Western Rivers: An Economic and Technological History* (Cambridge: Harvard University Press, 1949) 278. Lloyd M. Short, *Steamboat-Inspection Service: Its History, Activities, and Organization* (New York: Institute for Government Research, D. Appleton, 1922) 1–10.

6. For *Cist's Weekly Advertiser* study, see Hunter's *Steamboats on the Western Rivers*, Table 10, 278. The table also provides estimates of the financial cost of steamboat accidents. See also, Paul F. Paskoff, *Troubled Waters: Steamboat Disasters, River Improvements and American Public Policy, 1821–1861* (Baton Rouge: LSU Press, 2007) 19–23, 27–39.

7. Georgeann McClure, "Steamboat Disasters," http://iagenweb.org/history/rivers/Disaster_index. htm; Iowa History Project website, accessed January 6, 2014. Short, *Steamboat-Inspection Service*, 86–87, 104–105. Minnesota was located in the Fifth Supervising District (Galena, Illinois) of the inspection service, and later moved to the fourth.

8. St. Paul District, Corps of Engineers, *Old Man River: 50th Anniversary, Nine-Foot Navigation Channel, Upper Mississippi River, 1938–1988*, (St. Paul: Corps of Engineers, May 1998) 4–8. "Introduction," *Gateways to Commerce: the U.S. Army Corps of Engineers' 9-Foot Channel Project on the Upper Mississippi River*, US National Park Service website, http://www.nps.gov/history/history/online_books/rmr/2/intro.htm, accessed February 8, 2014. John O. Anfinson, "The Secret History of the Mississippi's Earliest Locks and Dams," *Minnesota History* 54 (Summer 1995): 260–262.

9. August B. Easton, *History of the St. Croix Valley*, vol. 1 (Chicago: H. C. Cooper, Jr. & Co., 1909) 516–519.

10. "Death and Ruin, Terrible Effect of the Cyclone at Lake Gervais Cottages," *St. Paul Dispatch*, July 14, 1890, 1. *St. Paul Daily Pioneer Press*, July 14, 1890, 1, 2. Mark J. Meister, "The Man Who Painted the Lake Gervais Tornado, *Minnesota History* 45 (Winter 1977): 329–331, Koester said his camera stood at Cherokee Avenue and Ohio Street.

11. "Two More Bodies," *Minneapolis Tribune*, July 15, 1890, 2. Meister, "The Man Who Painted the Lake Gervais Tornado," 329. Bruce F. Watson, *Weather Guide* (Navarre, MN: Freshwater Biological Research Foundation, 1976) 157.

Chapter One

1. Rodney C. Loehr, "Caleb Door and the Early Minnesota Lumber Industry," *Minnesota History* 24 (June 1943): 126–127. "St. Croix Boom Site," Washington County (MN) Historical Society Website, http://projects.wchsmn.org/reference/sites/boomsite/, accessed February 3, 2014. Mildred Hartsough, *From Canoe to Steel Barge on the Upper Mississippi* (Minneapolis: University of Minnesota Press, 1934), 118.

2. "Boys of the Militia," MplsT, July 13, 1890, 1. SPPP, July 15, 1890, 9.

3. SPPP, July 18, 1890, 1.

4. Harold Wills, "Pieces of Craft Scattered to the Wind," RWDRE, February 4, 1957, 1–2. Milt Davis, "Lives of More Than One Hundred Persons Lost in Lake Storm," undated newspaper clipping, copy in Goodhue County Historical Society's *Sea Wing* files.

5. Loehr, *Minnesota History* 24 (June 1943): 138–139.

6. "The Daily Pick Up," RWDR, July 12, 1890, 3.

7. *Pierce County Herald,* Aug. 6, 1890, 4. "Table IV: Population of Wisconsin, 1890, 1900, 1895," State of Wisconsin, *Public Documents of the State of Wisconsin*, vol. 2 (Madison, 1903) 138.

8. RWA, July 10, 1890, 4.

9. Information regarding the Niles and Wethern families is from August B. Easton, *History of the St. Croix Valley,* vol. 1 (Chicago: H. C. Cooper, Jr., & Co., 1909), 516–19. W. E. (Bill) Boyes (grand-nephew of Captain Wethern and his wife Nellie Boyes Wethern) to author, October 5, 1986, includes information on the family and photographs of the *Sea Wing*, copy in author's possession and Goodhue County Historical Society Collections. Gladys E. Camp, "Sea Wing Foundered 83 Years Ago," RWDRE, July 13, 1973, 1, 7.

10. Mrs. Francis Baker (daughter of Gartland), interview with author, April 17, 1983, notes in author's possession.

11. "The Preacher's Prophecy," RWDRE, March 19, 1971, 11. See also RWDRE, July 12, 1958, 11, the undated published account of the itinerant missionary, by *Sea Wing* clerk Ed Niles, was first reprinted here.

12. Ibid.

13. RWDRE, July 12, 1958, 11.

14. Wills, "Pieces of Craft Scattered to the Wind," RWDRE, February 4, 1957, 1.

15. "What Capt. Wethern Says," SPD, July 17, 1890, 1. Wills, "Pieces of Craft Scattered to the Wind," RWDRE, February 4, 1957, 1.

16. "The Preacher's Prophecy," RWDRE, March 19, 1971, 11.

17. Here and two paragraphs below, Easton, *History of St. Croix County*, vol. 1, 516–519 Information on the Wethern family is from this source. David Young Wethern, father of the *Sea Wing's* captain, married Esther A. Niles. One of Esther's brothers, Edwin Niles, also moved to Diamond Bluff where he and wife Eliza had six children including Edmond, William and Harry all of whom served as *Sea Wing* crewmen for their cousin David Niles Wethern. The three Niles brothers' sister, 16-year-old sister Millie Niles, was among those who died on the *Sea Wing*. Ellie Niles, another sister, married Mel Sparks, the ship's co-owner. Nellie Boyes, of Diamond Bluff, married David N. Wethern on October 22, 1876. Dallas W. Pritchett (grand-niece of Captain David Wethern) to author May 5, 1987, contains Wethern family information and photographs. Pritchett added genealogical background on the Wetherns in another letter to the author, August 31, 1990, photographs in Goodhue County Historical Society collections; letter in author's possession.

18. "The Local Pick Up," RWDR, July 12, 1890, 3.

19. RWDR, July 9, 1 July 10, 1.

20. *Winona Daily Republican,* July 14, 1890, 2. RWDR, July 9, 1890, 1; July 10, 1.

21. Trenton became a wood stop for steamboats in the early 1850s with Wilson Thing handling operations at Trenton Landing. Thing built a house near the landing that later became home to Benjamin and Elizabeth Way, parents of the Way children on the *Sea Wing*, see "Editorial Incidents of Trenton," *River Falls* (Wisconsin) *Journal*, June 15, 1876, 1, col. 3. Esther Ducklow of River Falls, provided notes, and news clippings to the author, Ducklow to author, October 13, 1990, in author's possession. Mattie Flynn was the daughter of Thomas and Mary McCusker Flynn of Trenton, Family files, Pierce County Historical Society, Ellsworth, Wisconsin. Dorothy Winjum (daughter of Myrtle and granddaughter of Allen and Sarah Adams), interview with author, July 27, 1983; Easton, *History of St. Croix County*, vol. 1, 519.

22. Mark Diedrich, "Red Wing: War Chief of the Mdewakanton," *The Minnesota Archaeologist* 40 (March 1981): 22–23. Frederick L. Johnson, *Goodhue County, Minnesota: A Narrative History* (Red Wing: Goodhue County Historical Society, 2000, 12–15, 84–86. Madeline Angell, *Red Wing, Minnesota: Saga of a River Town* (Minneapolis: Dillon Press, 1977) 31–32, 146. Jesse Rosenberger, *Through Three Centuries* (Chicago: University of Chicago Press, 1922), 298.

23. "Lake Pepin," Minnesota Department of Natural Resources website, http://www.dnr.state.mn.us/areas/fisheries/lakecity/pepin.html, accessed December 21, 2013.

24. Mathilda Staiger Metzler (sister of Frances and Annie Staiger), interview with author, 1983.

25. "New Made Graves," SPPP, July 16, 1890, 1; "Given Up by Pepin," SPPP, July 17, 1890, 1.

26. Elayne Galvin (granddaughter of William Schoeffler), interview with author, 1983. Easton, *History of St. Croix County*, vol. 1, 519.

27. "Capt. Wethern's Tale," *Minneapolis Journal*, July 22, 1890, 6.

28. Interview with Robert Joseph Carlson, grandson of G. A. Carlson, September 21, 1982, notes in author's possession. G. A. Carlson was the leading force in earning, for Red Wing, distinction as Minnesota's "Lime Center." Stone from the city's limestone bluffs was burned in kilns producing lime, needed for mortar. A. T. Andreas, *An Illustrated Atlas of the State of Minnesota* (Chicago: A. T. Andreas, 1874) 235–236. Johnson, *Goodhue County Minnesota*, 101–103. Angell, *Saga of a River Town*, 175, 350.

29. SPPP, July 17, 1890, 1.

30. Marcella Johnson (half-sister of Lenus Lillyblad) to author, September 12, 1983, letter in author's possession.

31. Mrs. Mary C. Leach, "Saved By Fate!" Newspaper clipping in Stockholm (Wisconsin) Institute Collection labeled "Minneapolis Centennial Issue, 1949." Gladys E. Camp, "Sea Wing Foundered 83 Years Ago," RWDRE, July 13, 1973, 1. Mary Leach, who gave this account to her daughter Gladys Camp, did not give her name before marriage. Two women named Mary (Kulstad and Nelson) were listed as missing the boat in Lake City.

32. Ibid.

33. Ed Schenach in undated RWDRE article in GCHS *Sea Wing* file. Ed Schenach and George Smith, both survivors of the *Sea Wing* disaster, were quoted in an undated Red Wing newspaper article about the disaster. Playing the bass was a part time job for Ed Schenach. He was a stonecutter by trade and often carved names on tombstones.

34. Camp, "Sea Wing Foundered 83 Years Ago," RWDRE, July 13, 1973, 1. Family members believe that the "Henry Rehder," listed as leader of the four-piece band on the *Sea Wing* was Claus Henry Rehder, a noted violinist in the area. Supporting that contention is an initial *St. Paul Pioneer Press* report of the accident on July 14, 1890, page 1, column 2 "High Sea of Waves," that notes the "two children of C.H. Rehder," among the dead. Claus Henry Rehder was father of Rosa and Johann Henry, both of who died in the accident; Cathie Rehder Heilemann to author, October 29, 1999, email, copy in author's possession.

Chapter Two

1. "At Camp Lakeview, the First Regiment Reviewed by Governor," *St. Paul Sunday Globe*, July 13, 1890, 1. "Boys of the Militia," *Minneapolis Tribune*, July 13, 1890, 1. RWDR, July 12, 1890, 3.

2. Frederick W. Ames, *Historical Sketch and Souvenir, Company A 1st Infantry*, not paginated. RWDR, Aug. 8, 1890, 3.

3. Camp, "*Sea Wing* Foundered," RWDRE, July 13, 1973, 1, 7. Leach, "Saved By Fate!" 1949 newspaper clipping in Stockholm (Wisconsin) Institute Collections.

4. Paul F. Paskoff, *Troubled Waters: Steamboat Disasters, River Improvements and American Public Policy, 1821–1861* (Baton Rouge: LSU Press, 2007) 19–23, 27–39. Rosenberger, *Through Three Centuries*, 298, 302.

5. George Smith in undated RWDRE article in GCHS *Sea Wing* file. RWDR, July 15, 1890, 3. Also aboard were E. D. Morris, C. D. Jacoby, C. S. Sultzer, and W. J. Eisenbrand.

6. "Lake Pepin's Horror," LCGS, July 15, 1890, 1.

7. "Hurled to Doom Without Warning," SPPP, June 13, 1926, 7, carries an interview with Captain Wethern in which he recalls the accident. Dolores Haustein Harris, "Writer's Grandfather Gives Firsthand Account of Historic Tragedy," *Generations of Today* (July 2000) 29–31, 42. The article is based on Casper "Cap" Haustein's 1929 account of the *Sea Wing* disaster. Haustein described the horse-drawn "buses".

8. Leach, "Sea Wing Foundered 83 Years Ago," RWDRE, July 13, 1973, 1.

9. *Minneapolis Journal,* July 22, 1890, 6.

10. "Death and Ruin, Terrible Effect of the Cyclone at Lake Gervais Cottages," *St. Paul Dispatch*, July 14, 1890, 1. "The Dead Recorded," *Minneapolis Tribune*, July 17, 1890, 1. "A Terrible Catastrophe," RWDR, July 14, 4.

11. Mark J. Meister, "The Man Who Painted the Lake Gervais Tornado," *Minnesota History* 45 (Winter 1977): 329–331. SPPP, July 14, 1890, 1. Bruce F. Watson, (Navarre, MN: Freshwater Biological Research Foundation, 1976) 157.

12. Harris, "Writer's Grandfather Gives Firsthand Account of Historic Tragedy," 30–31. SPPP, July 15, 1890, 1, 9.

13. Here and two paragraphs below, I. B. Woodward, editor, *Historical Sketch and Souvenir First Battalion Artillery NGSM, Battery A* (Minneapolis: Miller Printing, 1892) not paginated. Woodward's account

provides the best overview of the storm and its effect on Camp Lakeview. Leach in RWDRE, July 13, 1973, 1. "Writer's Grandfather Gives Firsthand Account of Historic Tragedy," 31.

14. *Minneapolis Journal,* July 22, 1890, 6. Charles Lidberg in undated RWDRE article in GCHS *Sea Wing* file. RWDRE, Mar. 19, 1971, 10. "Lake Pepin's Horror," LCGS, July 15, 1890, 1.

15. Milt Davis, "Lives of More than One Hundred [sic] Persons Lost in Lake Storm," unattributed copy of a newspaper article, GCHS *Sea Wing* file.

16. "Capt. Wethern's Tale," *Minneapolis Journal*, July 22, 1890, 6. SPPP, July 17, 1890, 1.

17. "Lake Pepin's Horror," LCGS, July 15, 1890 4. Davis in GCHS *Sea Wing* file. SPDG, July 18, 1890, 2.

18. RWDR, July 14, 1890, 3.

19. Ibid.

20. Metzler interview with author, July 2, 1983, notes in author's possession.

21. Camp, "Sea Wing Floundered," RWDRE, July 13, 1973, 1, 7. Leach, "Saved By Fate!" 1949 newspaper clipping in Stockholm (Wisconsin) Institute Collections.

22. Here and below, Woodward, *Historical Sketch and Souvenir* not paginated. Camp, "Sea Wing Floundered," RWDRE, July 13, 1973, 1, 7.

23. Woodward, *Historical Sketch and Souvenir* not paginated. "Among the Militia," SPPP, July, 15, 1890, 9.

24. "Lake Pepin's Horror," LCGS, July 15, 1890, 1. "High Sea of Waves," SPPP, July 14, 1890, 1. "Death's Toll," *St. Paul Dispatch*, July 14, 1890, 1. Metzler interview with author, July 2, 1983, notes in author's possession.

25. Davis, "Lives of More than One Hundred [sic] Persons Lost in Lake Storm." Camp, "Sea Wing Floundered," RWDRE, July 13, 1973, 1, 7.

26. "What Capt. Wethern Says," SPD, July 17, 1890, 1.Wethern interview in SPPP, June 13, 1926, 7.

27. Ibid.

28. Smith and Schenach interviews in GCHS *Sea Wing* file.

29. SPPP, July 16, 1890, 1. SPPP, July 23, 1890, 5.

30. "The Charge of Drunkenness," SPPP, July 16, 1890, 1. "His First Pleasure Excursion," SPPP, July 17, 1890, 1. "Capt. Wethern's Case," *St. Paul Dispatch*, July 15, 1890, 1. *Winona Daily Republican,* July 15, 1890, 2.

31. Wills, "Pieces of Craft Scattered to the Wind," RWDRE, February 4, 1957, 1–2.

32. Wethern interview in SPPP, June 13, 1926, 7. *Minneapolis Journal,* July 17, 1890, 1.

33. "The Preacher's Prophecy," RWDRE, March 19, 1971, 11.

34. George Diepenbrock interview in undated RWDRE article in GCHS *Sea Wing* file. "Lake Pepin's Horror," LCGS, July 15, 1890, 1. Davis, "Lives of More than One Hundred [sic] Persons Lost." "Beneath the Waves," SPPP, July 15, 1890, 1. RWDR, July 15, 1890, 3. SPDG, July 15, 1890, 4.

35. Davis, "Lives of More than One Hundred [sic] Persons Lost." "The Storm Began," SPPP, July 14, 1890, 1. "Beneath the Waves," SPPP, July 15, 1890, 1.

36. Wills, "Pieces of Craft Scattered to the Wind," RWDRE, February 4, 1957, 1–2.

Chapter Three

1. George Diepenbrock interview in undated RWDRE article in GCHS *Sea Wing* file.

2. Wills, "Pieces of Craft Scattered to the Wind," RWDRE, February 4, 1957, 2.

3. "Hurled to Doom Without Warning," Wethern interview in SPPP, June 13, 1926. 1, 7.

4. SPPP, July 17, 1890, 1 and July 15, 1890, 9. Roy Wethern interview in SPPP, October 18, 1959, 12.

5. SPPP, July 15, 1890, 9.

6. RWDRE, July 15, 1950, 1, Chellstrom reference from Metzler interview with author, July 2, 1983, notes in author's possession.

7. Davis "Lives of More than 100 [sic] Lost in Lake Storm," in GCHS *Sea Wing* file. "Notes of the Wreck," LCGS, July 15, 1890, 4.

8. "Hurled to Doom Without Warning," Wethern interview in SPPP, June 13, 1926, 7. "Fateful Funnel's Fury," SPDG, July 14, 1890, 1.

9. Metzler interview with author. Lampman and Stevens related the story of the Staiger drownings to the family.

10. "Hurled to Doom Without Warning," Wethern interview in SPPP, June 13, 1926, 7; RDWS, July 16, 1890, 1. Davis, "Lives of More than 100 [sic] Lost in Lake Storm," in GCHS *Sea Wing* file, p. 2.

11. Schenach interview in GCHS *Sea Wing* file.

12. Harry Mabey interview in Davis, "Lives of More than 100 [sic] Lost in Lake Storm," in GCHS *Sea Wing* file.

13. Julia Wiech Lief to author, April 15, 1987, letter in author's possession. Lief noted details of Fred Scherf's losses. Lidberg and Smith interviews in GCHS *Sea Wing* file. PCH, July 16, 1890, 4.

14. SPPP July 16, 1890, 1. Mabey interview in Davis article, GCHS *Sea Wing* file.

15. Richard Truttman (nephew of Charlie Truttman) interview with author, May 22, 1983. "The Storm Began," SPPP, July 14, 1890, 1.

16. "Jumped and Swam Ashore," SPPP, July 14, 1890, 1. "The Barge the Safer Place," SPPP, July 16, 1890, 1. Mabey interview in Davis article, GCHS *Sea Wing* file.

17. Baker interview with author. Lidberg interview in GCHS *Sea Wing* file. Schenach interview in RWDRE, July 13, 1960, 1.

18. Richard Truttman interview with author, May 22, 1983. SPPP, July 15, 1890, 1. RWA, July 17, 1890, 4.

19. Smith interview in GCHS *Sea Wing* file. Davis in GCHS *Sea Wing* file. Schenach discovered he was near Florence Township, found his brother who was visiting nearby, and got a ride to Frontenac to catch the train to Red Wing. He jumped off before the train stopped when he saw the crowd at the Red Wing depot. "I didn't feel like talkin' and explainin'," he said in an interview at age 95, RWDRE, July, 13, 1960, 1.

20. Davis in GCHS *Sea Wing* file, 2. LCGS, July 15, 1890, 1. RWDR, July 14, 1890, 3. Woodward, *Historical Sketch and Souvenir First Battalion Artillery NGSM, Battery A,* not paginated.

21. RDWS, May 28, 1890, 4 (news brief on new Lake Pepin steamer, the *Ethel Howard,* based at Lake City). "Why He Refused," SPPP, July 17, 1890, 1.

22. "Lake Pepin's Horror," LCGS, July 15, 1890, 1. "Very Climax of Terror," SPDG, July 15, 1890, 1. RWDR, July 14, 1890, 3.

23. "Hurled to Doom Without Warning," Wethern interview in SPPP, June 13, 1926. Red Wing, Lake City, and St. Paul newspaper accounts, July 14, 15, 1890.

24. "The Storm Began," and "Battle with the Elements," SPPP, July 14, 1890, 1.

25. SPPP, July 16, 1890, 9. In this account Perry corrected some glaring mistakes, including an exaggeration of the number of people they rescued, in a report published by the newspaper the day before. See also "Heroism of a Few," SPDG, July 15, 1890, 1.

26. Ibid.

27. RWDR, July 15, 1890, 3. SPPP, July 16, 1890, 1. Davis in GCHS *Sea Wing* file.

28. Wills, "Pieces of Craft Scattered to the Wind," RWDRE, February 4, 1957, 2. RDWS, July 16, 1890, 1 *Minneapolis Journal,* July 22, 1890, 6. Edmund Burke is credited with helping Wethren to shore. The first edition of the book reported "Ed Hall" and was in error, see "Hero of Sea Wing Disaster In 1890 Dies," RWDR clipping in author's possession. Eugene H. Burke to author August 21, 1983, letter in author's possession.

Chapter Four

1. "Lake Pepin's Horror," LCGS, July 15, 1890, 1. "The Reaper," and "Sad Scenes," *Minneapolis Journal,* July 14, 1890, 1. RDWS, July 16, 1890, 5.

2. Milt Davis, "Lives of More than One Hundred [sic] Persons Lost in Lake Storm," unattributed copy of a newspaper article, GCHS *Sea Wing* file. "Dead Excursionists" and "High Sea of Waves," SPPP, July 14, 1890, 1.

3. "The Lake of Death," and "Seeking for Friends," SPPP, July 15, 1890, 1. "They Hear No Call," and "Carried Home," RWDR, July 15, 1890, 1. "Very Climax of Terror," SPDG, July 15, 1890, 1. SPD, July 14, 1890, 1.

4. Here and below, "Harris, "Writer's Grandfather Gives Firsthand Account," *Generations of Today,* (July 2000) 31, 42. "Among the Dead," RWDR, July 15, 1890, 1.

5. Here and below, "Carried Home," RWDR, July 15, 1890, 1. "Recovering the Dead," SPD, July 16, 1890, 1.

6. "Drowned! An Awful Disaster on Lake Pepin, Minn." MplsT, July 14, 1890, 1. RDWS, July 15, 1890, 5. "Harris, "Writer's Grandfather Gives Firsthand Account," 41–42.

7. George Smith in undated RWDRE article in GCHS *Sea Wing* file in GCHS *Sea Wing* file. "Harris, "Writer's Grandfather Gives Firsthand Account," 42.

8. "Maj. Pierce's Efforts," SPD, July 18, 1890, 1. Red Wing businessman Arthur Pierce was the first captain of Company G when it was organized in 1883. He was a First Regiment Staff Officer at the time of the accident, Curtiss-Wedge, *History of Goodhue County,* 1018–1019. SPDG, July 15, 1890, 4. Adjutant General Mullen also told of the Guard's work at Central Point in his *Biennial Report* (Minneapolis: Harrison and Smith, Printers, 1891) 6.

9. "Taken from the Wreck," SPPP, July 15, 1890, 1. Mabey interview in Milt Davis, "Lives of More than One Hundred [sic] Persons Lost in Lake Storm," unattributed copy of a newspaper article, GCHS *Sea Wing* file. SPPP, July 15, 1890, 1.

10. Mabey interview in Davis article in GCHS *Sea Wing* file. "The Barge the Safer Place," SPPP, July 16, 1890, 1. "Lake Pepin's Horror," LCGS, July 15, 1890, 4.

11. "Death's Path," SPD, July 14, 1890, 1, "Recovering the Dead," SPPP, July 16, 1890, 1.

12. Ibid.

13. "High Sea of Waves," SPPP, July 14, 1890, 1. SPDG, July 15, 1890, 4.

14. "A Mournful Day," SPPP, July 16, 1890, 1.

15. Horace Anderson (son of Carl Anderson) interview with author, September 16, 1983. Swedish immigrant C. O. Anderson, a teamster, had worked in the stables of the King of Sweden.

16. "City of the Dead," SPDG, July 15, 1890, 4. "Sad Scenes," *Minneapolis Journal*, July 14, 1890, 1. RDWS, July 16, 1890, 5. RWA, July 17, 1890, 4.

17. Office of the Adjutant General, "Annual and Bi-annual Reports, 1869–1924," 1890 Muster Rolls, 39, contains the Company G roster at the time of the accident. SPD, July 14, 1890, 1. RDWS, July 16, 1890, 1.

18. "Brave Militiamen in Role of Grace Darlings," SPDG, July 15, 1890, 1. RDWS, July 16, 1890, 1. SPPP, July 15, 1890, 1.

19. "The Shore Nearest the Wreck," SPPP, July 15, 1890, 1.

20. SPPP, July 15, 1890, 9.

21. RDWS, July 16, 1890, 1. See St. Paul *Pioneer Press* photo on page 63 for an image of National Guardsmen at work on the wreckage of the *Sea Wing*.

22. "Work of Recovery," and "Another Floated to the Surface," SPPP, July 15, 1890. 1. "Recovering the Dead, SPD, July 15, 1890, 1.

23. "Another Floated to the Surface, SPPP, July 15, 1890, 1. "Brave Militiamen in Role of Grace Darlings," SPDG, July 15, 1890, 1. *In Memory of Those Who Perished*, 2.

24. SPD, July 14, 1890, 1. SPPP, July 15, 1890, 9. Woodward, *Historical Sketch and Souvenir First Battalion of Artillery NGSM, Battery A*, not paginated.

25. Ibid.

26. "Fastened to the Bodies," SPPP, July 15, 1890, 1. "Patrolled Constantly," SPPP, July 16, 1.

27. *Those Who Perished*, 2. "Fastened to the Bodies," SPPP, July 15, 1890, 1.

28. "Scene at the Wreck," and "Work of Recovery," SPPP, July 15, 1890, 1. Adjutant General John Mullen lived in Wabasha, just downriver from the accident, and commuted to the accident scene.

29. "Beneath the Waves," SPPP, July 15, 1890, 1. Winona *Daily Republican*, July 14, 1890, 1.

30. Here and below, "The Number of Passengers," SPPP, July 16, 1890, 1.

31. "Dynamite Exploded," SPPP, July 16, 1.

32. RWDR, July 15, 1890, 3.

33. "Given Up By Pepin," SPPP, July 17, 1890, 1. Red Wing City Council, Book E, 317–18. Councilman George Cook, a Red Wing representative at Central Point, was in the process of creating a clay-based sewer pipe during the summer, laying groundwork for a major city industry.

34. SPPP, July 15, 1890, 9. See also "Beneath the Waves," subhead: "Sad Experiences," July 15, SPPP, 1.

35. Ibid.

36. "The Time of the Wreck," SPPP, July 15, 1890, 1. "A Mournful Day," SPPP, July 16, 1890, 1.

37. "Brave Militiamen in Role of Grace Darlings," SPDG, July 15, 1890, 1. "Dynamite Employed," SPPP, July 16, 1890, 1.

38. SPPP, July 15, 1890, 2.

39. "City of the Dead," SPDG, July 15, 1890, 1. "A Mournful Day," SPPP, July 16, 1890, 1. *Those Who Perished*, 2. District Court (Goodhue County), Coroner's Records, 1867–1975, see "Coroner's Reports, 1890," Minnesota Historical Society, St. Paul.

Chapter Five

1. "Seeking for Friends," SPPP, July 15, 1890, 1. SPD, July 15, 1890, 2.

2. "Dynamite Employed," SPPP, July 16, 1890, 1.

3. RWDR, July 15, 1890, 3. "Patrolled Carefully," SPPP, July 16, 1890, 1. *Those Who Perished*, 2.

4. "City of the Dead," SPDG, July 15, 1890, 4. "Mournful Day," SPPP, July 16, 1890, 1. "A Day of Funerals," SPD, July 15, 1890, 1. "The Bells Toll," *Minneapolis Journal*, July 15, 1890, 1.

5. Ibid.

6. Metzler interview with author, July 2, 1983, notes in author's possession. Harris, "Writer's Grandfather Gives Firsthand Account of Historic Tragedy," 29–31. Cap Haustein references visits to Gottlieb and Catherine Persig, of Hay Creek, who also lost two daughters, Julia and Anna, on the *Sea Wing* and Fred Hattemer's family, like the Staigers, from Florence Township.

7. H. W. Keller to W. J. Crawford, July 15, 1890, transcription in Goodhue County Historical Society collections.

8. Leach, "Sea Wing Foundered 83 Years Ago," RWDRE, July 13, 1973, 7. This account does not give Minnie's last name, but the only Red Wing victim of that first name was Fisher.

9. "The Charge of Drunkenness," SPPP, July 16, 1890, 1.

10. "The Number of Passengers," SPPP, July 16, 1890, 1. RWDR, July 16, 1890, 3.

11. "The Charge of Drunkenness," SPPP, July 16, 1890, 1. The report suggests that Wethern ordered women and children into the cabin and cites a witness that supported that contention.

12. "Is He in Durance?" SPDG, July 16, 1890, 1. "The Number of Passengers," SPPP, July 16, 1890, 1.

13. "Man at Fault," SPPP, July 15, 1890, 4. "The Investigation," *Minneapolis Journal*, July 17, 1890, 1.

14. Ibid.

15. "The Charge of Drunkenness," and subtitle "Captain was Not Only Sober," SPPP, July 16, 1890, 1. "Is He to Blame?" SPDG, July 16, 1890, 4.

16. Ibid.

17. "Lake Pepin's Horror," LCGS, July 15, 1890, 1, 4.

18. RWDR, July 14, 1890, 3.

19. "Floating Near Shore," and "Listing the Missing," SPPP, July 16, 1890, 1–2.

20. SPPP, July 16, 1890, 2, Rikka Vieths' full name, "Friedrika, "is in the Official Records of Ministration of St. John's Lutheran Church, Book II, p. 257. This book written in German, lists the St. John's members lost in the disaster.

21. "The Inquest," SPPP, July 16, 1890, 1. "The Inquest," RWAS, July 16, 1890, 2. Franklyn Curtiss-Wedge, "Arland H. Allen," in *History of Goodhue County, Minnesota* (Chicago: H. C. Cooper, Jr. & Co., 1909) 748.

22. "The Inquest," SPPP, July 16, 1890, 1. "The Inquest," RWAS, July 16, 1890, 2. Red Wing lawyer Frank Wilson, 45 in 1890, had served as both city and county attorney.

23. Ibid.

24. Ibid.

25. "Consideration by the Grand Jury," SPPP, and "The Charge of Drunkenness," SPPP, July 16, 1890, 1. SPD, July 15, 1890, 1.

26. SPD, July 16, 1890, 1.

27. "Patrolled Constantly," SPPP, July 16, 1890, 1. The crew of Red Wing workers remained at the site.

28. "Given Up By Pepin," and "Bloated and Blackened," SPPP, July 17, 1890, 1.

29. "Given Up By Pepin," SPPP, July 17, 1890, 1. "Placed in One Box," "In Search of Missing Bodies, and "The Body of His Son," SPPP, July 17, 1890, 1.

30. Roy Anderson interview with author, September 22, 1983, copy in author's possession.

31. Marcella Lillyblad Johnson to author, September 12, 1983, letter in author's possession. Lenus Lillyblad was a half-sister to Johnson.

32. "Assist the Searchers," SPPP, July 17, 1890, 1. The original 1986 edition of *The Sea Wing Disaster* and the 1990 reprint erroneously reported the names of Johanna Humpert's parents. They were Christ and Sophie Schulenberg. The Schulenberg family retains its deep ties to Red Wing and continues to honor the memory of the relatives lost in the accident.

33. "Assist the Searchers," SPPP, July 17, 1890, 1. Dorothy Winjum (daughter of Myrtle and granddaughter of Allen and Sarah Adams), interview with author, July 27, 1983.

34. "Placed in One Box," SPPP, July 17, 1890, 1. Caleb Johnson, a descendant of the Meros, email to author, March 17, 2014, and March 18, 2014. Family genealogist Johnson notes, Susan Mero and her children were Mayflower descendants "many times over: from John Alden, William/Alice/Priscilla Mullins, Myles Standish, George Soule, Henry Samson, Edward Doty, and Richard Warren." Johnson also contributed family photos and Fred Mero's telegram found in the narrative.

35. "Bloated and Blackened," SPPP, July 17, 1890, 1.

36. Ibid. The story cited above provides information on the identification of John Strope's body.

37. "Assist the Searchers," SPPP, July 17, 1890, 1.

38. Ibid.

39. Ibid

40. Edna Martenson and Myrtle Martenson (nieces of the Persig sisters) interview with author, February 3, 1984. RDWS, July 14, 1890, 2. SPPP July 17, 1890, 1. "Assist the Searchers," SPPP July 17, 1890, 1.

41. "The Body of His Son," SPPP, July 17, 1890, 1. Robert Carlson (grandson of G. A. Carlson), interview with author, September 21, 1982, notes in author's possession.

42. "Ninety-Nine Dead," STP, July 17, 1890, 1.

Chapter Six

1. "On Pepin's Shores," *Minneapolis Journal,* July 16, 1890, 1. "Governmental Inspection," SPPP, July 17, 1890, 1. "Lake Pepin's Horror," LCGS, July 15, 1890, 4.

2. Ibid.

3. "Steamboat Inspection: The New Rules and Regulations for the Examination of Steam Boilers, Additional Guarantees for the Safety of Passengers," notes requirements for adjustable life preserves "made of good, sound cork blocks [at least six pounds] with belts and shoulder straps attached," *New York Times*, September 1, 1871. SPD, July 18, 1890, 4.

4. "Govermental Inspection," SPPP, July 17, 1890. Wethern reported 187 cork and tule life preservers. Winona *Daily Republican,* July 16, 1890, 2.

5. "A Statement from Capt. Wethern," SPPP, July 17, 1890, 1. In regard to safety equipment on the barge *Jim Grant*, the following regulation was in effect: Rule III.—Life Saving Appliances, Section 18, page 101. Section 20 applies to barges in tow of steamers, thus, pertaining to the barge *Jim Grant*, being towed by *Sea Wing*. It requires 25 life preservers, 10 buckets and three axes. It is not known if the *Grant* was so equipped. Supervising Inspector-General of Steam Vessels, *Laws Governing the Steamboat Inspection Service*, as amended January, 1882-'83-'84-'87 (Washington: Government Printing Office, 1887).

6. "The Investigation," *Minneapolis Journal*, July 17, 1890, 1. "A Statement from Capt. Wethern," SPPP, July 17, 1890, 1.

7. "Capt. Wethern's Case," SPD, July 16, 1890, 1. Hugo J. Herder, 25 at the time of the accident, was a clerk at Red Wing's C. E. Friedrich & Co.

8. "His First Pleasure Excursion," SPPP, July 17, 1890, 1. *Minneapolis Journal,* July 17, 1890, 1.

9. RWDR, July 16, 1890, 3.

10. "What Capt. Wethren [sic] Says," SPD, July 17, 1890, 1. The newspaper account lists one crewman as "West Willie." The name should be W. W. Willey.

11. "An Explanation," LCGS, July 22, 1890, 5. "Why He Refused," SPPP, July 17, 1890, 1.

12. "Capt. Wethern's Case," SPD, July 16, 1890, 1. *Minneapolis Journal*, July 22, 1890, 6. RWA, July 24, 1890, 1.

13. "What Capt. Wethren [sic] Says," SPD, July 17, 1890, 1.

14. Ibid.

15. Ibid.

16. "Tolling Church Bells," SPPP, July 17, 1890, 1. RDWS, July 23, 1890, 2. RWA, July 24, 1890, 1.

17. RWDR, July 17, 1890, 3.

18. "It was a Mournful Day," SPPP, July 16, 1890, 1. SPDG, July 15, 1890, 4. *Those Who Perished,* 3. RDWS, July 23, 1890, 2.

19. RDWS, July 23, 1890, 2.

20. RWDR, July 17, 1890, 3.

21. The breakdown of Arland H. Allen is prominent in the recollection of Red Wing citizens and was mentioned by Art Saupe (who attended school with Allen's daughter), Mathilda Staiger Metzler, Roy Anderson and Horace Anderson during 1982 and 1983 interviews with author. Mathias and Katrina Kayser moved to Red Wing in 1865. He went into the furniture business two years later. Mathias was 55-years-old at the time of the *Sea Wing* disaster. The Kayser's furniture store building still exists, at this writing. In 1915 it was remodeled into Ahler's Flats, a West Third Street apartment building. Information on Kayser is from Fred Kayser (grandson of Mathias) interview with author, July 22, 1986, notes in author's possession. James S. Brisbin, *Souvenir of Red Wing, Minnesota* (Red Wing: Red Wing Printing Co., 1891). See also Angell, *Saga of a River Town*, 195.

22. RWA, July 17, 1890, 4.

23. RWDR, July 17, 1890, 3. SPPP. July 18, 1890, 1. SPD, July 17, 1890, 1.

24. RWDR, July 18, 1890, 3.

25. Ibid.

Chapter Seven

1. *Minneapolis Journal,* July 22, 1890, 6. RWDR, July 19, 1890, 3.

2. SPPP, July 20, 1890, 8.

3. RWDR, July 22, 1890, p. 6.

4. *Minneapolis Journal,* July 22, 1890, 6.

5. RWA, July 24, 1890, 1. SPPP, July 23, 1890, 5. It is not known whether St. Paul river pilots James A. Ritchie and P. F. Ritchie were related.

6. SPPP, July 23, 1890, 5.

7. Ibid.

8. Ibid.

9. *Those Who Perished,* 3. "Memorial Services For Those Who Perished Upon Lake Pepin, July 13, 1890," program for the July 25 *Sea Wing* disaster commemoration in Red Wing.

10. Ibid. The Sheldons, Mary and Theodore, both New Englanders, moved to Minnesota Territory's Red Wing in 1856. He became deeply involved in the city's post-Civil War emergence as a manufacturing center. Mary Sheldon died in November 1891; he died nine years later, Franklyn Curtiss-Wedge, *History of Goodhue County, Minnesota* (Chicago: H.C. Cooper, Jr. & Co. 1909) 31–32.

11. Ibid. RDWS, July 13, 1890, 4.

12. "The Local Pickup," *Red Wing Republican,* August 21, 1890, 3. RWDR, July 29, 1890, 3. Schenach interview in GCHS *Sea Wing* file. Baker interview with author. New York state-born James D. Kellogg moved to Red Wing in 1868 and established a photography business. He was 51-years-old at the time of the *Sea Wing* disaster, *History of Goodhue County* (Red Wing: Wood & Alley, 1878) 522.

13. *Those Who Perished,* 7.

14. Ibid.

15. Ibid.

16. Ibid. RWDR, July 29, 1890, 3. RDWS, July 30, 1890, 4.

17. RWDR, July 19, 1890, 3. C. A. Rasmussen, *A History of the City of Red Wing, Minnesota* (Red Wing: Published by author, 1934), 295. Curtiss-Wedge, *History of Goodhue County, Minnesota,* 96–97.

18. *Those Who Perished,* 32–33.

19. Ibid.

20. Angell, *Saga of a River Town,* 114, 126. Jennison, a Harvard graduate wounded at Nashville while leading the Tenth Minnesota Regiment against the Confederates, had been Minnesota governor Alexander Ramsey's secretary at the outset of the war. See John Imholte, *The First Volunteers* (Minneapolis: Ross E. Haines, 1963) 6–9.

21. *Those Who Perished,* 9.

22. SPPP, July 26, 1890, 1, 5.

23. Ibid.

24. SPPP, July 29, 1890, 5.

25. Ibid.

26. RWDR, August 19, 1890, 3.

27. "It Condemns Wethern, the Report of the Investigation of the Sea Wing Disaster Loosed from Red Tape," SPPP, August 23, 1890, 10. RWA, August 21, 1890, 1. SPPP, August 23, 1890, 10.

28. "Captain Wethern Censured," RWA, August 27, 1890, 1. "It Condemns Wethern," SPPP, August 23, 1890, 10.

29. SPD, July 17, 1890, 1. RDWS, Aug. 27, 1890, 1. SPPP, August 23, 1890, 10.

30. RWA, Aug. 28, 1890, 4.

Chapter Eight

1. SPPP, August 23, 1890, 10. RDWS, August 27, 1890, 1. "It is Found that the Sea Wing Carried 204 Passengers," *Minneapolis Tribune,* July 22, 1890, 3.

2. "Hurled to Doom Without Warning," Wethern interview in SPPP, June 13, 1926, 1, 7. Lidberg and Smith interviews in GCHS *Sea Wing* file.

3. Author interviews with Horace Anderson, Saupe and Metzler.

4. Here and below, SPD, July 17, 1890, 1. SPPP, August 23, 1890, 10. RDWS, August 27, 1890, 1.

5. US Treasury Department, Steamboat Inspection Service, *Report of the Board of Supervising Inspectors of Steam Vessels* (National Archives T 38.10:1891) Washington DC: 1891, 83.

6. Here and below, Easton, *History of the St. Croix Valley,* vol. 1, 516–519. "Hurled to Doom Without Warning," Wethern interview in SPPP, June 13, 1926.

7. Don O'Grady, "Ol' Man River," SPPP, October 18, 1958, 12, interview with Roy Wethern.

8. RDWS, July 23, 1890, 7, August 27, 1890, 2.

9. Red Wing City Council, Book E, 317–318.

10. Galvin interview with author. Johnson letter to author.

11. Curtiss-Wedge, *History of Goodhue County*, 706, 1002. W. F. Toensing, *Minnesota Congressmen, Legislators, and Other Elected Officials* (St. Paul: Minnesota Historical Society, 1971) 48, 98.

12. RWDA, August 7, 1890, 2. RDWS, August 13, 1890, 5.

13. Willard, Annual Report of the City Clerk, *Financial Statement*, year ending April 30, 1891.

14. Robert Joseph Carlson interview with author, September 21, 1982. Carlson emphasized G. A. Carlson's depressive behavior and its affect upon his surviving son, Theodore.

15. Here and below, Nils P. Haugen Papers, St. Croix Valley Research Center, University of Wisconsin-River Falls. The postscript refers to President Cleveland's struggles with Congress as the financial Panic of 1893 progressed. Haugen indicates Wethern, was among "sick Dems" [Democrats] in his district, "Nils Haugen," Govtrack.us website, https://www.govtrack.us/congress/members/nils_haugen/405220, accessed March 2, 2014.

16. Easton, *History of the St. Croix Valley*, vol. 1, 520. Records in the "Local History Files" of John Norquist, Diamond Bluff.

17. Metzler interview with author, July 2, 1983.

18. Twenty-three-year-old Martin Scherf had been nursed back to health by his mother following a severe bout of typhoid fever and was on the *Sea Wing* celebrating his survival, Mildred Scherf interview with author, June 11, 1987.

19. Notes from the O'Shaugnessy Family Tree indicate that Martin O'Shaugnessy's father was born in County Galway and his mother came from Balbriggin near Dublin, Coleen A. Schaffer to author, July 16, 1990, original in author's collection.

20. Here and below, Esther Ducklow of River Falls provided notes and news clippings related to Trenton and the Way family to the author, Ducklow to author, October 13, 1990, in author's possession. See also "Editorial Incidents of Trenton," *River Falls* (Wisconsin) *Journal*, June 15, 1876, 1.
At the time of the first edition of this book, Dorothy Winjum, a descendant of Allen and Sarah Adams, parents of three young *Sea Wing* victims, kept records for the picturesque Trenton cemetery. Her mother, Myrtle Adams, then nine, had not gone along with her siblings and cousins on the *Sea Wing*, PCH, December 14, 1893, 1.

21. Rasmussen, *History of Red Wing, Minnesota*, 295.

22. E. J. [Eliza Jane] Crawford to Willie (My Dear Brother), May 7, 1890, copy in the GCHS *Sea Wing* files.

Epilogue

1. Here and below, "A Meteorological Look at the Sea Wing Disaster," a 1990 manuscript by Thomas A. Hodgson, copy in author's possession. Hodgson has worked in yacht race management as a professional and volunteer.

2. Here and below, Roy W. Meyer, *The Ghost Towns and Discontinued Post Offices of Goodhue County*, Red Wing: Goodhue County Historical Society, 2003, 73–73. Haines and Dean, Haines, C. J. and E. G. Dean. *A Souvenir of Lake City, Minnesota Including Frontenac, Villa Maria and Rest Island*, (Lake City: H. A. Young & Co and Jewell Nursery, 1897) 24–28. "Hok-Si-La Municipal Park," Wildlife Viewing Areas website, http://www.wildlifeviewingareas.com/wv-app/ParkDetail.aspx?ParkID=513, accessed March 8, 2014. Ericson, Kathryn, *Map of Goodhue County, Minnesota* (Red Wing: Warner & Foote, 1877) 16.

3. Here and below, "A Survivor's Experience," *St. Paul Dispatch*, July 22, 1890, 4. "St. Paul News: None of the Witnesses Examined Blame Capt. Wethern," Minneapolis *Tribune*, July 25, 1890, 3, "Mr. Webb is [sic] gentleman who so gallantly rescued Miss May Casey and he graphically described their struggle in the water up to the time they were picked up by a sailboat." No sailboats were out in the dangerous waters of Central Point picking up victims, but Corp. B. F. Perry and Wesley Hills, working from a rowboat, did pick up some survivors.

4. Mathilda Staiger Metzler interview with author, July 2, 1983, notes in author's possession. Her two older sisters died on the *Sea Wing*. Horace Anderson interview with author August 27, 1982; his father was teamster Carl Oscar Anderson, who brought *Sea Wing* victims to undertaking parlors. Art Saupe, "Notes Pertaining to the *Sea Wing*," April 11, 1983, manuscript, copy in author's possession. Fred Kayser interview with author, July 22, 1986, notes in author's possession.

5. John Norquist interview with author, March 17, 2014, notes in author's possession. Easton, *History of the St. Croix Valley*, 520.

6. H. W. Keller to W. J. Crawford (Dear Brother) July 15, 1890, copy in Goodhue County Historical Society *Sea Wing* files. E[liza] J. Crawford to Willie (My Dear Brother), May 2, 1890, copy in Goodhue County Historical Society *Sea Wing* files.

7. C[hristian] A. Rasmussen, *A History of Goodhue County, Minnesota* (Red Wing: Self-published, 1935) 295.

Index